# Developing the Credit-based Modular Curriculum in Higher Education

# Developing the Credit-based
## Modular Curriculum in
## Higher Education

Mick Betts
Robin Smith

FALMER PRESS
Taylor & Francis Group

**UK**     Falmer Press, 1 Gunpowder Square, London, EC4A 3DE
**USA**   Falmer Press, Taylor & Francis Inc., 325 Chestnut Street, 8th Floor, Philadelphia, PA 19106

---

First published in 1998

**A catalogue record for this book is available from the British Library**

ISBN 0 7507 0890 5 paper

**Library of Congress Cataloging-in-Publication Data are available on request**

.

Jacket design by Caroline Archer

Typeset in 10/12 Garamond by Graphicraft Limited, Hong Kong

*Printed in Great Britain by Biddles Ltd., Guildford and King's Lynn on paper which has a specified pH value on final paper manufacture of not less than 7.5 and is therefore 'acid free'.*

*Every effort has been made to contact copyright holders for their permission to reprint material in this book. The publishers would be grateful to hear from any copyright holder who is not here acknowledged and will undertake to rectify any errors or omissions in future editions of this book.*

# Contents

*Contents*

# List of Figures

# Acknowledgments

We acknowledge the contributions made by members of the University's Centre for Accreditation and Negotiated Awards (UCANA) especially the late Mike Taylor, Lyn Brennan, Karen Dobbyn, Christopher Harris, Bob Mercer and Stephanie Williams who have been important to us in formulating and testing our ideas. We would especially like to thank Lyn Brennan, Sue Betts and Chris Collins who undertook to read early drafts of the text and made helpful and constructive suggestions for improvement, and Bob Mercer for two of the case studies.

We would also like to thank Anglia's Media Production Unit, especially Ann Scott for the production of the original diagrams, and Jenny Knight for her help with the preparation of the text.

Crown copyright is reproduced with the permission of the Controller of Her Majesty's Stationery Office.

# Chapter 1

# Introduction

In the 21st Century *knowledge* will become increasingly less valuable and prized as the currency of education. The separation between knowledge and *learning* will become wider. Technology will make access to knowledge easier than ever before, for more people than ever before. It will become the role of Higher Education (HE) to provide higher order learning skills as well as, and eventually rather than, knowledge of subject disciplines. Of course, it has always been more valuable to be able to say what a poem might mean than to recite it, but in a knowledge and information-rich world these skills of analysis and interpretation will be at a higher premium. The implications of this for teachers in HE are far reaching. The knowledge transmission model will be dead. The CD Rom and other digital devices will be the source of much knowledge and information. The need for the teacher's role to become one of mediator, mentor, listener, facilitator, interpreter and critical friend will be real and pressing. As Barnett states when reviewing the profound changes that have occurred in university education:

> There are not one or two but multiple knowledges. Process knowledge, tacit knowledge, action learning, experiential learning. All these terms point to the multiplication of our ways of knowing in the modern world. The point is not that the sites of knowledge production are proliferating; it is that the academy's definitions of knowledge are increasingly challenged. (Barnett, 1997, p. 3)

Those who express contempt, confusion or professional insult at having their teaching role described as above will nevertheless have to become practitioners of this approach, if not advocates of it. They may take comfort however that such an approach rescues education from its recent past concern with imposing facts, and liberates the teacher and student by requiring a creative engagement with those facts and a renewed seeking out of that knowledge. In 1854, through Mr Gradgrind, Dickens in *Hard Times* satirized the value of an obsession with 'facts' in education. Facts were all the lumpen proletariat could manage. At the threshold of the 21st century, aiming as we are at mass participation in HE, we should perhaps re-appraise the situation. Credit accumulation and transfer systems, or CATS as they are often referred to, and the parallel curriculum framework based on modular systems are part of that re-appraisal. In many ways they liberate the student and teacher, in other ways they constrain them.

In the UK, Credit-based Modular Systems (or CBMS as we will call them throughout) have been created through a fragmented and inconsistent process of piecemeal development. For good practical reasons they were developed by deconstructing the traditional curriculum model of higher education rather than by building a new system from bottom up. The British system of higher education (HE) has not been particularly receptive to modular systems and credit accumulation and transfer. For many, indeed, most universities, which have adopted CBMS, the change is very recent. The credit-based modular curriculum system, has at its heart a revolutionary approach to HE. Revolutionary, that is, for the UK system, which for 800 years has been designed not with flexibility in mind or student choice, but to be tutor centred. It is based on the principle of an elite club which only a few can be allowed to join. In the UK Higher Education has for many years been the territory of the privileged few. Participation rates remained no more than 7 per cent in the 1960s.

Degree programmes were governed by certain strictly adhered to principles. Degree study was predominantly full-time. Part-time modes were parallel forms of full-time programmes taken by students who for some reason had failed to capitalize on the opportunities offered at 18. In England, degrees were three years long (or occasionally longer if they included the need for additional study as in the case of work placements or languages). In Scotland they were four. The time element was important. In the UK system, standards related to pace. Students were expected to gain their degrees within a 'normal' period of time. Any longer demonstrated that the student had failed to achieve the desired standards. On the other hand the rarer part-time degrees were lengthy affairs, often six years, doubling the time needed for the full-time degree, demonstrating there was no easy or backdoor route into the graduate club.

Much changed during the 1970s, but many traditional attitudes remained. Many of the dilemmas to which this book makes reference stem from the attempts to place upon the rigid, traditional HE culture of the UK an educational philosophy which stresses flexibility. Most developments in the modular curriculum were initiated in the polytechnics, such as Oxford. It is hardly surprising that the initiative came through that route. The polytechnics had no traditions, but they did have a shared mission based upon the common control and ownership by the local educational authorities. They had a need to serve the community, especially the local community. Their importance to the business environment was emphasized. They embraced a wider range of provision including sub-degree programmes through BTEC and a strange new two year programme called the Dip HE. They also started to introduce a greater range of part-time provision. They had in the Council for National Academic Awards (their validating and awarding authority) an organization that facilitated debate, unhindered by the labyrinthine concerns of university senates. The CNAA was flexible in its approach to curriculum development, was engaged with the international community, including the USA, and open in its deliberations. At the same time, the Open University (which started in 1972) was breaking new ground in terms of the intended student body and the way it served its learners through its unique method of delivery. Again, flexibility, breaking down tradition and taken for granted ways of approaching the academic world, became a key factor in its success. Like the polytechnics and the CNAA, the OU had to fight prejudice, and its students had to wait many years before their degrees were ranked as equivalent to the 'proper' degrees of the university sector generally.

These debates are still playing themselves out now but the backdrop has changed. The 30 per cent or more participation rate that is now aimed for has introduced a mass education system. More significantly, the nature of the intake has changed. As Gareth Williams identifies, statements relating to the 30 per cent participation rate are often based on the involvement in full-time higher education of young people usually in the context of degree study. If part-time and more mature individuals are considered then 'the probability of any individual entering higher education is nearly double this figure' (Williams, 1997, p. 4). Mass participation has brought a call for diversity. Business, industry and the professions have become key players and consumer choice has become important, not just in HE but within society generally. Accountability has also become a watchword, so much that was hidden and cosy in HE has now had to be made explicit. The credit-based modular curriculum reflects this new approach to UK life. It emphasizes more explicit outcomes in relation to each small part of the degree, rather than the more broadly defined 'course' in general. There is a more closely articulated relationship between these outcomes, the levels of achievement and assessment. There is greater student autonomy in constructing the programmes and a greater range of entry gates and exit points. All this is a long way from the traditional three year degree programme designed by university staff for the 18-year-old with three 'A' levels.

In the 1990s, institutions were faced with the need to develop more flexible, faster and cheaper ways of meeting the needs of the growing number of students. They started to develop modular programmes based on credit accumulation systems in parallel with, or based on, existing curriculum frameworks. It has been claimed that 90 per cent of institutions have adopted the modular or unitised curriculum (HEQC, 1996a) but these vary considerably in their nature and the extent to which they are modular or, more importantly, have the key design features of CBMS. According to work undertaken as part of the Graduate Standards Programme, only 7 per cent of universities are still 'predominantly linear', 26 per cent are unitized or partially so, and 67 per cent are modular or partly modular. Some 60 per cent of universities claim to have become modular or unitized since 1992 and 80 per cent of institutions claim to have established credit frameworks (HEQC, 1997a). These figures cover up a multitude of sins, however. The predominant British model of HE has been that a few students enter a few institutions and are taught, over a fixed period, a programme of study predominantly determined by the authors of the content (the tutors) and are then subject to an assessment to determine the extent to which the knowledge has been successfully imbibed. Credit accumulation and transfer systems and modular systems require a programme of study that is not necessarily time-based, is periodically assessed, is transparent in its outcomes and reflects the shift of influence from the tutor to the student. A model which reflects much more an open USA ethos rather than the closed British one. Modular and credit-based courses had their origins in the USA for much the same reason that they developed a century later in the UK. As Theodossin states:

> In the latter part of the nineteenth century pressures grew to replace the uniform classical curricula with something more suited to contemporary needs. At a philosophical level, there was a growing acceptance of student-centred learning and of John Dewey's advocacy of self realisation achieved through study fitting the individual's interest. There was also increasing demand for courses of a practical nature relevant to the real world. (Theodossin, 1986, p. 5)

Thus in the UK an evolutionary approach has been taken. Existing models were adapted incrementally. It would not, of course, have been possible to start with a blank sheet of paper either within individual institutions or nationally. However, many of the dilemmas now faced in CBMS institutions derive from the failure to appreciate the extent to which CBMS and its underpinning philosophy represents radical change which requires sophisticated change management. However, the reality has been drip feed development and crisis management. The mismatch and clash between the still predominant old culture and the attitudinal changes required to underpin CBMS, requires effective strategies to enable transition from one curriculum model to another within an institution. However good the transitional arrangements within specific institutions, there remains a significant group of dilemmas that arise because those institutions must remain in a system which is uncomfortable with itself and has not adjusted to the new mass higher education system in the UK.

This book focuses on these dilemmas. Whilst it aims to describe some of the more common approaches to CBMS from a practical stance, to enable those who wish to follow the CBMS path to identify the various options open to them, it also attempts, in addition, to do what in the authors' view has been lacking in the literature written by enthusiasts for CBMS. This is to identify in an explicit manner the inherent dilemmas that are created by CBMS approaches and to recognize that certain of the issues arising from these dilemmas have no single or simple solutions. Much of where we are now is still uncharted territory. Institutional culture and value systems to underpin CBMS have yet to be developed. Too often the enthusiasts for credit-based modular programmes within universities (and we count ourselves amongst these) have stormed ahead developing their guidelines, regulations and systems and left the vast majority of colleagues bobbing along in their wake. There are many questions that still need to be asked. Not all of them have answers, but they are nevertheless important if reluctant credit accumulators and modularizers are going to be convinced that it is worth entering into dialogue. CBMS still has a long way to go before it gains acceptance amongst many opinion leaders in higher education and before it becomes the universal curriculum model that enthusiasts seek for it. It will not achieve this goal by steam rolling its way forward. We must recognize that the UK credit-based modular systems are based on a philosophy that has it roots only a few inches below the surface. It runs counter to a HE philosophy and ideology that withstood the test of time. Financial pressures are making the introduction of a mass UK HE system more problematic. If we want HE to be driven by a clear educational philosophy, rather than by the forces of the market, then the debate required to arrive at a consensual view needs to be brought into the foreground.

The older ideology still has some powerful adherents. Debates about standards, i.e. the *lowering* of standards in HE, have given opponents of new fangled innovations imported from the alien US culture greater opportunity to denigrate. Many of the issues currently facing HE, however, are pertinent irrespective of CBMS. The introduction and growth of CBMS has often served to direct attention away from the issues *per se* or has exposed flaws in the traditional systems which have been in existence for many years and which have nevertheless been associated with the problematic nature of CBMS. The dubious, inconsistent and arbitrary practices of the universities' examinations boards are now exposed through the transparency of the CBMS assessment system. The difficulty of establishing comparability between subject disciplines and institutions, the weaknesses of the external examiner system and the precarious nature of the classification system have all been present for many years. CBMS did not create them, it exposed them. It is important to draw out these issues, and face them rather than hoping that they will go away or that time will bring capitulation from one side or the other.

The credit-based modular system represents a fundamental and revolutionary change to the HE curriculum. It cannot be grafted on to the existing institutional practices piecemeal. It sits uncomfortably within the existing national structure. The move towards CBMS requires changes in organizational systems, procedures and frameworks. Most importantly, it requires changes in organizational and national culture. This is not easily achieved. Fullan (1991) suggests that we need to be supported in changing even in the direction of change to which we subscribe. Support can be given more easily if dilemmas are public, subject to real discussion and real consultation and acted on accordingly. The motivation for writing this book came out of a sense of unease about the way the discussion and consultation were being conducted. We had a sense that organizations such as some of the newly established consortia were rail-roading the supporters of CBMS into compromises without the dialogue and agreement that is required if real change is to occur and if recalcitrant colleagues are to be convinced. Dearing's unworkable qualifications framework (Dearing, 1997, p. 143) is a clear example of the dangers of closed consultation as we discuss in Chapter 9.

The early enthusiasts of CBMS were operating in a context very different from the 1990s. Modular courses were rare in the UK. The binary divide between autonomous universities and the less prestigious local authority controlled polytechnics was very concrete, and credit accumulation was a novel concept.

Against this background the advocates were faced not just with educational issues but political problems. CBMS, as the period since its introduction has demonstrated, has been a remarkable lever towards innovation in many different areas. Certainly it undermined many long held conventions in the academic world. The predominant CBMS model adopted in the UK of undergraduate programmes being rated at 360 credits made up of modules at three levels, was an understandable response to accommodate the conventional academic world. It also helped to introduce CBMS with the minimum of fuss and without the perceived need for protracted debate. The education world has moved on. The explosive nature of CBMS in challenging long held assumptions is now readily visible. The time has now come to review where we are and seek to find solutions to dilemmas based on curriculum and pedagogic principles rather than structural and political ones.

Credit-based systems of education offer the opportunity to 'the system' to take advantage of many innovations which governments (of all shades) seek to encourage. As Kennedy recognizes in the context of Further Education:

> Education and training must become much more flexible in order to meet the needs of those in under represented groups. There should be a national framework of credit for further education. . . . This framework will provide accreditation for interim achievement. Learners will be able to chart their learning gain, get recognition for their work and build up credit through their lives. (Kennedy, 1997, p. 86)

Similar sentiments have been expressed by Dearing in the context of HE (Dearing, 1997). CBMS provides a platform for a range of flexible approaches. Credit-based systems can foster in-company accreditation for example, and thus build upon company-based training and facilitate the development of a highly skilled and well educated work force (see Chapter 5). The processes of the Accreditation of Prior and Prior Experiential Learning (APL/APEL) encourage individuals to build upon past success and therefore maximize potential and gain credit for what has already been achieved (see Chapter 6). The system acts as a magnet moving a static workforce towards higher levels of skill and qualification. APL/APEL has provided the single most important means of providing accelerated awards. These factors have enabled larger numbers of students from all walks of life and age groups to move through the higher education system in a way that in comparative terms is much cheaper than under the older regime. Credit-based modularity enables the design of programmes to meet *students'* needs, thus moving the curriculum from the supply side (what universities want to deliver) to the demand side (what students and their employers identify as what they want). We must not underestimate the radical change that this represents. We must prepare for the impact on resource management, staffing, employment contracts, facilities' management, student recruitment, guidance, support and a whole range of related matters.

However, universities that have adopted the reality rather than the rhetoric of the CBMS philosophy find themselves falling foul of a variety of systems and processes that are deeply ingrained within the HE psyche and are also reinforced by government's lack of real understanding of the true potential. Bringing the Department of Education together with the Department of Employment has not yet demonstrated a mind set that can really appreciate and encourage development. Universities with traditional missions fare better in the league tables than those which are most innovatory because the league tables are built upon implicit missions which hark back to the 1950s and beyond. The lack of progress in developing true measures of 'value added' has allowed those institutions that have missions which do not fully accord with the philosophy underpinning CBMS to continue to thrive, while those that do not struggle for recognition and resources. This is a particularly sharp irony in a government inspired culture that has espoused the concept of 'value addedness' so vehemently. Funding methodologies have not yet identified credit as their base (although there has been much talk for a long time) and external quality bodies fight shy of really tackling credit-based systems.

Credit-based modular systems are not value free. Conventionally, higher education has been covered in a cloak of mystery. Examination boards and marking systems have been shrouded in the mysteries of professional secrecy. However, CBMS requires a more open and explicit approach to all areas of the assessment process, from the explicit outlining of module outcomes to the establishment of clear criteria for their assessment. Teachers are also required to consider how to structure teaching and learning activity in order that out-comes might be achieved and measured through the assessment. Students on CBMS programmes become aware very quickly of the rules governing the game and are therefore able to challenge the taken for granted mores of institutions. They can manipulate their learning and manage their achieve-ments. They become the subject of the educational process rather than the passive object of it. Once you allow for greater openness and choice you begin to allow the student to challenge the almost divine right of academic authorities in matters of once holy writ. This has far reaching effects not just upon staff within the university but upon others who have traditionally sought to control the curriculum.

Chief amongst these are the professional bodies. It is not possible to generalize about the reactions of the professional bodies to CBMS, but few have embraced the developments with enthusiasm, although many are begin-ning to see that CBMS is here to stay and may indeed have something to offer. The negative reaction was much to do with a philosophy, held for a long time, that to reach professional goals the student must be constrained to cover a more rigid and often allegedly more rigorous syllabus. What is more, this syllabus is sequentially progressive and therefore the order as well as the content, becomes inviolable. This view has led some universities to distort the nature of their CBMS (and indeed traditionally constructed) programmes rather than challenge the long held beliefs that the professional body is always right. Clearly, the professional bodies have the power to refuse accreditation and this has meant that such challenges have had to be carefully approached.

However, the climate is changing as more universities recognize the need for CBMS programmes for institutional survival. This recognition is beginning to have an impact on the professional bodies, even the most conservative ones, although it is not without precedent for staff to misrepresent the views of the professional body in order to frustrate CBMS policy development within their own institution!

In many areas flexible credit-based modular programmes are beginning to be attractive for the purpose of continuing professional development (CPD), allowing busy professionals to construct their own programmes best suited to their individual professional needs. Professional bodies are beginning to wake up to the fact that if they are to achieve their in-service goals, such flexible programmes are crucial. Modularity and credit accumulation provide the backbone to such developments for them. Crucially, the flexibility of credit-based modularity enables dynamic continuous development of the curriculum that defines a professional area, and the professional recognition that goes with it. Modularity enables incremental review and gives to professional bodies a context and structure for research (ideally in partnership with the universities). It is, after all, in everyone's interest that the 'licence to practise' that professional body recognition confers is up to date, thereby increasing the employability of the graduate and enhancing the status and reputation of the companies represented in the professional body area. The explicit use of learning outcomes, fundamental to CBMS, brings to vocational areas a level of detail relating to professional *competencies* that conventional syllabi rarely achieved or aimed for. Under CBMS, professional bodies can feel more secure that the professional skills that they seek to guarantee are explicitly focused upon, whereas in traditional programmes there is the danger that these outcomes can be submerged within the important concerns of the university for intellectual rigour, with its emphasis on theory and knowledge-based success. Modular programmes, which emphasize continuous assessment and therefore diversity of assessment practices, encourage institutions to move away from the traditional examination which fails to access or assess, in any direct measure, many of the professional skills. CBMS programmes encourage innovatory methods of assessment directly linked to the learning outcomes identified within the module. Skills such as report writing, interpersonal communications, practical and group skills all become amenable to direct measurement. While programmes measured by end of year examinations and professional body examinations run the risk of granting a licence to practise on the 40 per cent of 40 per cent model i.e. an examination which requires a pass mark of 40 per cent from an examination paper which covers only part of the syllabus (see below). Continuous assessment against explicit learning outcomes makes the granting of professional body recognition a more predictable, representative and quality assured process (see Chapters 3 and 4).

There could, of course, be the accusation that such approaches whilst protecting the interests of the professional body undermine what is truly *higher* in higher education, the ability to identify relevant theory and knowledge and apply it to a particular case. This has been the attack on the National Council for Vocational Qualifications[1] and the introduction of National Vocational Qualifications especially as they move into undergraduate and postgraduate areas of HE. Here again credit-based modularity can counter this. Because of the transparency of outcomes, module developers are confronted with the question, 'What is credit being awarded for?' This requires them to make plain the development of theory and knowledge outcomes in a precise way and indicate the articulation with the related skills required for success. For this reason, NVQs can be embedded within so called academic modules but cannot of themselves be awarded higher education level *academic* credit.

Professional bodies are one special kind of awarding body. There are numerous other bodies such as the English National Board for Nursing and Midwifery (ENB), City and Guilds and Edexcel Foundation (previously BTEC), that make awards for programmes of study that either result from a fixed syllabus followed by an institution or which give recognition to a syllabus devised 'in-house'. Some of these bodies are powerful, others are small and often obscure. Nevertheless they all have a view about the worth and equivalence of their own awards, and therefore the national and institutional debates about credit worth and level impinge upon their interests. It must remain the individual university's responsibility to determine the credit value of an external award rather than the awarding body itself, since it is in the interest of the awarding body to grant itself as much credit at whatever level that it can muster. Indeed we argue later that this same principle (that of the separation of those responsible for course design from those responsible for the awarding of credit) should operate within institutions themselves as part of their quality assurance processes (see Chapter 7). The dilemma facing a university, and indeed the sector as a whole, is that without a national or regional framework providing general credit rating, individual awarding bodies can play one institution off against another seeking the best deal and then confronting institutions with a *fait accompli*, daring the university to weaken its recruiting position by under rating the candidate with a particular award. (The university willing to give a BTEC, HND 240 credits being a more attractive proposition to a student or employer who might be paying than one willing to grant only 180).

We believe that credit-based modularity, unlike traditional time-based HE, provides the tools to help arrive at logical equitable decisions about equivalence. *Learning outcomes* can be easily mapped against those of comparable awards and thus an equivalence against a *volume* of credit is relatively straightforward. Similarly when *level* is judged against explicit criteria rather than obscure or ill defined notions of maturation, decisions can be shown to be fair and consistent. Consistency, if not uniformity, must be achieved not just within an establishment but between universities nationally and ultimately internationally. This would suggest that national approaches through consortia of universities are something that must be encouraged. Robertson's attempt through 'Choosing to Change' (Robertson, 1994) and the South East England Consortium for Credit Transfer 'Guideline' (SEEC, 1996) are impressive attempts to produce some agreement in a higher education credit-based modular jungle that has grown like Topsy. However, there is a danger that such approaches will reinforce a prevalent trend in the late 1990s to remove the autonomy from universities and replace it with a centralized national curriculum. The development of higher level NVQs dominated by the lead bodies and lacking academic content and the introduction of a national curriculum for school teachers are cases in point. Establishing a framework for CBMS could become a own goal if by this we mean an attempt to produce a conformity of approach requiring eventually a common system of credit and module definition. As we show in later chapters, such attempts ignore the very real practical and philosophical difficulties. Although it is clear in this book that we favour certain solutions to the problems we identify, we also recognize that institutions operate in, and will continue to operate in, very different contexts. Solutions are often context specific and we must be on our guard when faced with *absolute* solutions especially since the debate has hardly started. Higher education is important to the development of a society because it values diversity. Through diversity comes creativity. National frameworks are worthwhile if they seek, not conformity but consistency. In our view credit transfer remains possible even with diversity, provided there is agreement about the exchange mechanism in use and the rates of exchange to be employed. This is the only way to approach this issue, since even if some national agreement came about it is very unlikely that international agreement will ever be forthcoming.

During the late 1980s and early 1990s consortia such as the South East England Consortium for Credit Transfer (SEEC) and The Northern Universities' Consortium for Credit Accumulation and Transfer (NUCCAT) were established with a view to facilitating transfer between higher education centres. Similar bodies exist in Scotland, Wales and Northern Ireland. They were based on a belief that there would be a market for such transfer as populations became more mobile and more knowledgeable about centres of excellence. The development of flexible CBMS itself encouraged enthusiasts to take this view. It was a philosophy based on a system rather than a system based on a philosophy. Some transfer has occurred. It is true that where students, usually mature in-service students, move employment and locality, transfer is eased. It has also allowed such students, and to some limited extent full-time students, the possibility of intermitting their studies without serious damage to their progress.

Financial realities in the current climate might make this a more appealing prospect and likely development. However, for the vast bulk of part-time and full-time students the ease of transfer has not made a significant difference. This is because the funding of HE has gone in the opposite direction to the ideology of flexibility. Thus universities, far from encouraging movement (even where there are universities in the same locality) are anxious to hold on to their students and not lose funding. Additionally, funding is encouraging students more and more to remain at home and therefore the option of moving to a university at some distance, let alone several universities on a serial basis is declining. Writing in 1986 Theodossin (1986, p. 43) was able to say that 'one may describe credit transfer activity in Britain as still limited and tentative'. Ten years later it was still the case. It may be possible that in the future we may discover students spending some time away and then on a planned basis, or out of circumstance, deciding to transfer to their local home-based institution for financial reasons. Transfer consortia have taken on new roles. They are concentrating more on staff development, research, identifying good practice, and through their guidelines, leading the sector towards producing a greater consistency.

We have deliberately pitched this book at two levels. We have on the one hand gone into detail at a very simple and practical level about the nature of CBMS. Thus we focus on areas like, credit, volume, level and so forth. For the experienced or committed CBMS individual this might not appear important. However, we feel it is necessary not only to describe the alternative models for those newly entering the debate, but to establish a basis to undermine some of the taken for granted assumptions of the 'experts'. Our second aim is to engage in the debate itself and to draw attention to the fact that practitioners of CBMS have an obligation both to establish a culture of continuous improvement and to develop a consensus view on how the sector might influence the debate on a national framework for qualifications and credit (Dearing, 1997; SEEC, 1996).

This book, therefore, is intended to be of interest to both those who recognize themselves to be substantially involved in the current debates about CBMS and those who are less expert but wish to enter the debate, perhaps within their own institution, as curriculum designers or institutional managers. For this reason we have written the book in such a way that the more experienced reader will be able to enter the debate at a more sophisticated level by commencing at Part 2, with a passing reference to the more descriptive elements in Part 1. However, even in Part 1 where we set up some of the basic elements of CBMS, we have attempted to raise some of the dilemmas that have to be confronted in curriculum design. Part 2 considers the practical issues that arise in implementing the various models for CBMS discussed in Part 1. In particular it considers the opportunities for flexibility that CBMS offers in the context of the quality and standards debate.

**Note**

1  Now the Qualifications and Curriculum Authority.

*Part 1*

# *The Universal Curriculum*

In this part of the book we provide a relatively simple introduction to the various models that can be adopted by institutions when developing the credit-based modular curriculum. It is primarily descriptive and intended for relative newcomers to the debate. It provides an introduction to the kinds of flexibilities that can be achieved and some of the dilemmas that must be confronted and resolved when determining the nature of the modular system to be adopted, including issues of module size, level, credit weighting and organization.

*Chapter 2*

# Patterns of Provision

At the heart of CBMS is the potential for flexibility. It provides an opportunity within an institution to make use of a module across a range of different degree courses, to build new courses quickly from an existing stock of modules and to provide differentiated routes within a degree programme. Similarly, if the institution so wishes it can provide courses which allow students to make a substantial amount of choice about the nature of the course they wish to be on. CBMS is adaptable to the different needs and contexts of institutions. There is a continuum of different patterns of CBMS based on degrees of course flexibility and student choice. All students start their educational career with a theoretically blank curriculum which needs to be filled in (Figure 2.1).

The question is the extent to which this is filled in by the institution and tutors or by the students themselves. Theodossin (1986, p. 14) identifies seven institutional mechanisms that can be used by a university to restrict the freedom of students to choose:

- requirements: essential modules for a programme
- prerequisites: completion of one module before another
- graded levels: certain levels available only at certain points
- sets, streams, series or co-requisites: modules offered as a package
- special permission: offered only after interview by special arrangement
- exclusion: restricted in access for one reason or another
- non availability: restricted on practical grounds such as timetabling.

Most CBMS institutions use these devices, albeit under different headings and to different degrees. The extent of usage, as a structured aspect of the institution's curriculum, allows us to propose several models. The various models that may be adopted within CBMS can be categorized as follows, which we discuss in turn:

Contained Provision
Boundaried Provision
Combined Model
    Major/Major
    Major/Minor
    Multiple combinations
Negotiated Provision

*Figure 2.1:* The student starts with a blank curriculum which needs to be filled

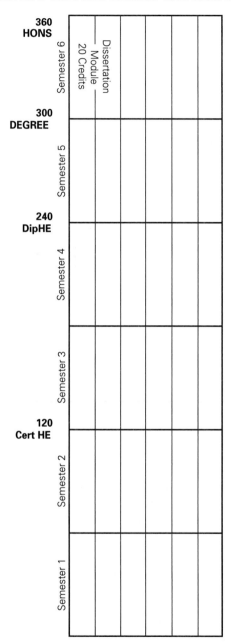

### Contained Provision

There are courses which are genuinely CBMS based in the sense that they are made up of modules of equal size and value delivered within a common time frame, assessed within that time frame and built upon the assessment principles of CBMS, but designed with very limited or no choice for students. The use of

*Figure 2.2:  Contained provision BSc (Hons) building*

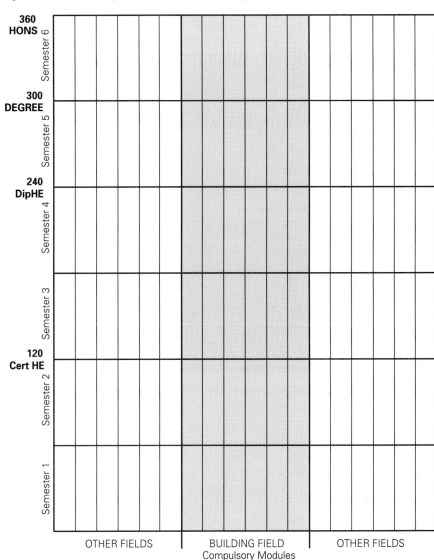

the modules is restricted to a specific cohort of students. This contained CBMS course is often the first stage towards greater flexibility in the future, or the response of an institution to professional body concerns and requirements which limit the amount of flexibility within the curriculum. Indeed this is little more than a single subject degree, and modularization adds very little to the curriculum beyond facilitating future change.

There are variations on this contained model. Within such a degree programme greater choice is sometimes given to the student through the use of 'designated choice modules' as well as compulsory core modules. The significance here is that, although choice is opened up and the greater flexibility which is possible under CBMS can be capitalized upon, the choice is limited to those modules which the *institution* decides are important rather than the *student.* Thus for example the student might register on a CBMS degree in English and be required to study only English but, as is also common with traditional programmes, be given some choice about what aspect of English to specialize in via options. In reality, therefore, this kind of CBMS adds little of value to the programme. Credit is in fact largely irrelevant, and some would argue that if there are no real benefits then the disadvantages of CBMS programmes outweigh the advantages. (See Figure 2.2)

### Boundaried Provision

A second CBMS model which we call the Boundaried model widens choice beyond the particular subject area for the student, but again within tight constraints. This model is often developed through departmental or faculty modular *schemes* which allow the student to select option modules from other cognate areas within the faculty. Here the emphasis is still largely on the single subject focus, but an opportunity is given to the student and taken by the course designers to look outside the subject for modules which the course designers see as relevant for the subject. These are often put on a list of appropriate options. Thus a student of history might be allowed to select modules from the English degree which focus for example on the literature of a particular period. This is a significant step down the flexibility road since, if it is to work effectively, the English and history staff and especially the timetablers will need to start talking to each other. Of course it is not unusual for such schemes to operate theoretically, but in practice the lack of coordination prevents any real choice or at least severely restricts it. If the process is real, different subject teams will need to coordinate matters at a level which hitherto might have been unusual. Thus for example the English team cannot set examinations on a particular date without first having checked that the historians have not set the same date! More problematic is the coordination of workloads to ensure that a student is not deluged unprofitably with work because they are doing more than one subject.

Figure 2.3: Boundaried provision BA (Hons) English

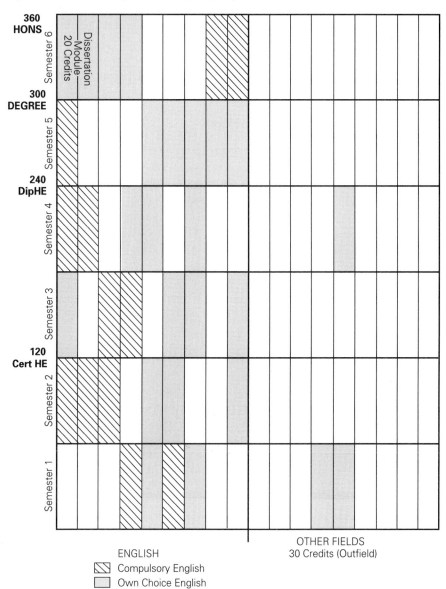

**Combined Model**

These problems of coordination are relatively easy to solve within the limitations of the Boundaried model since choice is still restricted and controlled by the institution. As soon as we decide to give students more choice outside these limited horizons then the key factor to come into play is how the flexible curriculum is to be organized and managed.

### Major/Major

A further development of the Combined model is for the 'optional' modules which are selected to be allowed to amount to the same, or nearly the same,

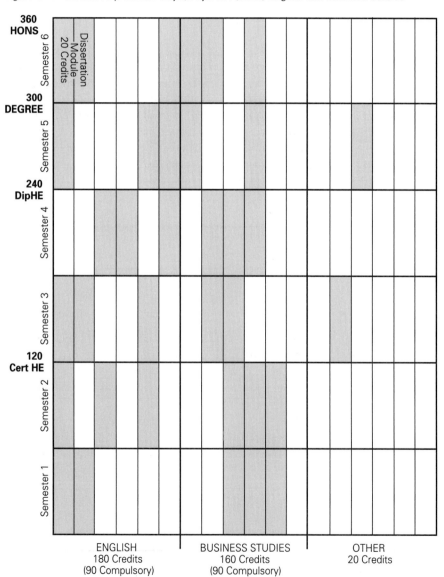

Figure 2.4:  Combined provision major/major BA (Hons) English and business studies

proportion as the original subjects are, so the student in fact has two almost equally weighted areas of study and a degree in English *and* history, or say business and law, is formed. Such Combined programmes are quite common but they can vary between institutions according to the degree of control that an institution wishes to place upon the student. Thus they may be restricted to schemes within faculties, so that combinations are within cognate areas, or at the other extreme the institution may be sufficiently well organized in terms of timetabling, student counselling and IT provision to allow students a genuine choice across the whole range of provision so that an individual might decide to take English and biological sciences. A number of crucial questions then need to be confronted which we outline below when discussing the Major/Minor combination, but essentially these relate to the amount, level and timing of modules and credits taken in order to achieve the Major/Major combination. Special problems arise in relation to the dissertation that a student may be required to do. If the dissertation is seen as fundamental to the demonstration of attainment in the specialist field and the student has two specialist fields, does this require two dissertations, a dissertation that integrates both fields (difficult with English and biology) or does one specialist field have to sacrifice its demand for the dissertation on practical grounds? There is not a single answer, but the debate between academics in resolving the policy draws out some interesting assumptions about the nature of their subject and of degree studies!

### Major/Minors

Within the Combined Model, schemes can also allow the student (i.e. it is the student who decides) to combine substantial amounts of work from another area as a Minor Route. The student could therefore get a degree in English *with* history or say business studies *with* law. We call this the Major/Minor Combination in which a student takes the majority of credits from a main or major discipline, and some other credits in lesser proportion from another. The crucial issue therefore that an institution must determine, is how many credits the student must have to retain the status of a Major, and how many must be retained in order to secure the subject title of the Minor in the award title. There are no fixed answers beyond, of course, the general agreement that there are more credits in the Major than the Minor.

The questions that are often put are as follows. Does the timing and level of the credit make a difference? In other words should the student always do more credits in the Major towards the end of the programme or is it legitimate for the major credits to make up the bulk towards the earlier part of the programme. More often than not the credits for the Major are felt to take on added significance if the student continues studying them right up to the end of the course and is not seen to drop them too early. There is no real need to take this view, since in CBMS modules studied at a particular level and credits gained for those modules retain their worth whenever they are studied.

*Figure 2.5:  Combined provision major/minor BA (Hons) English with business studies*

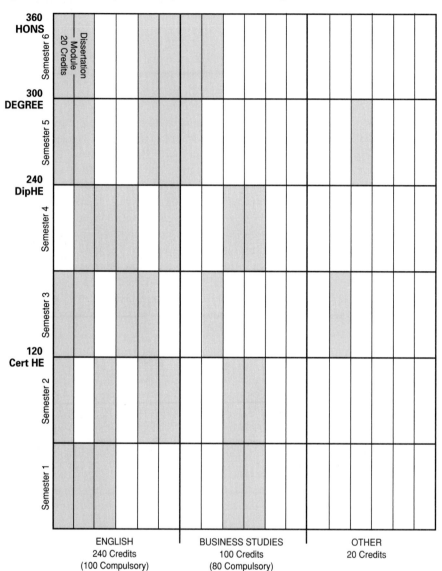

However, there remains an emotional attachment to the idea that pattern of study is somehow significant, which results from the attempt to introduce CBMS against the background of the traditional UK ethos. Should a greater proportion of the Major credits be from the higher level modules? Again there are no right answers but conventionally the answer has been that maintaining credibility in the Major does require a sustained effort in the higher level modules. There is some logic in this since the idea of a Major implies a level of expertise and therefore higher level study than a Minor, which has connotations of not having been studied as much or in such depth. Should a student's dissertation always be in the Major area as a defining aspect of Major provision? Similar arguments apply here. The dissertation is often defined as the culmination of the student's work and therefore to claim expertise without having undertaken a major piece of work in the area is often seen as unsatisfactory. This does, however, beg a few questions which could lead to other possible scenarios. For example, there is no reason why in a Major/Minor approach the dissertation should not be designed to require the student to focus attention on both areas of study. This might be possible where there is close correspondence between the subject areas. It also requires of the supervisory staff and student skills which are, perhaps, beyond their reach. What is the proportion of credit required to retain the Major designation and what is the balance that is required for the Minor? Can these be varied according to subject area or is a uniform framework required? The issue is one that stimulates great debate since some academic areas argue that in order to retain their title there are key and fundamental aspects of the course (sometimes backed up by professional bodies) that cannot be ignored, and this is what sets the parameters and must therefore be agreed by colleagues in other areas of the university. Of course if this becomes academic defensiveness then the model shifts back, through the process of debate, to the Boundaried model rather than the Combined.

A solution to some of the problems underpinning the questions and which retains the academic and professional integrity of a subject area, is to provide parameters within which selections can be made. Thus, for example, the regulations might say that in order to retain a Major dimension a student must do no less than say 160 credits of which 100 must be at a certain level, and to achieve a Minor, the credits must be no less than $x$ and no more than $y$ at certain levels. The dissertation must focus on the Major area but may integrate the Minor area, etc.

### Multiple Combination

Of course within these Major/Major and the Major/Minor models variations are possible, including choice of optional modules outside the original two areas of English and history. This opens up the possibility of degree titles of the kind that look like A *and* B *with* C or A *with* B *and* C as well as A *and* B or A *with* B! Much depends on the degree of flexibility that an institution wishes to introduce into course structures and the extent to which it feels that the degree title needs to reflect content. This brings us to the issue of transcripts which we discuss in Chapter 8.

With such Multiple Combination approaches, precisely the same issues arise, except the answers become more complex. Thus for example in relation to all three models (Major/Major, Major/Minor, Multiple Combination) the

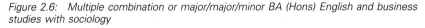

*Figure 2.6: Multiple combination or major/major/minor BA (Hons) English and business studies with sociology*

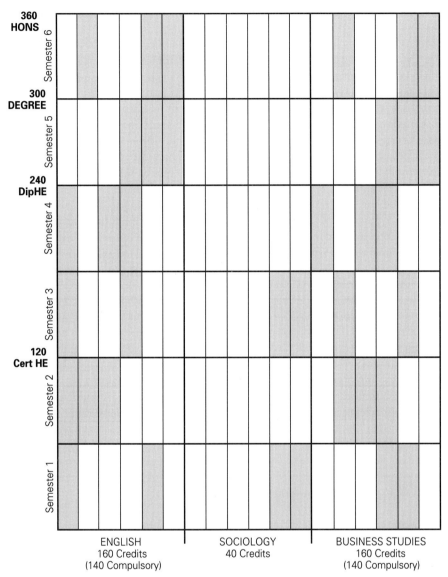

issue of how best to classify the student's degree becomes an issue. Does a student for example need to achieve an upper second class result in all subject areas in a combined programme in order to get an upper second? Is there a difference between a Major/Major combination and a Major/Minor? Can a student on a Minor route afford to be less successful and still achieve a First and if so what is the rationale for this? In other words, we get to the tricky issue of how you aggregate across different subject areas and get a result that is meaningful. Different institutions will find different solutions to these issues. The key point however is that in seeking solutions they will be confronted with a debate that the academic community has been trying to avoid and is at last being made public by the Graduate Standards Programme (HEQC, 1997b). That is, different subject disciplines have different traditions which define approaches to classification, that there is no real agreement about what it means to be a graduate let alone an upper second class graduate. This transparency is we believe to be applauded although alas the need to confront such issues has led some to criticize CBMS for past inadequacies now coming to light.

### Negotiated Provision

Inter-faculty schemes such as those described above are usually rule bound. Students are restricted in the amount and variety of choice they are permitted to make within and across subject disciplines. Such restrictions are made on the basis of practicality (an institution cannot timetable every possible combination of subject) and on academic judgments of what is 'proper'. Combining Animal Behaviour with Optical Management, for example, is likely to be ruled out on the grounds of lack of coherence in the programme! These academic considerations are based around the notion of standards which we look at more closely in Chapter 4, but it is important that we focus on one final development in UK credit-based modular systems, the growth of the Negotiated Award which represents the most flexible end of the continuum.

We will use the Negotiated award as the basis for later discussions in Chapter 5 about CBMS flexibility and standards because it represents the biggest challenge to conventional academic thinking. It is the kind of CBMS approach which critics disparagingly refer to as the 'cafeteria degree'. The Negotiated Award capitalizes upon the credit-based modular structure of the institution by allowing students to select modules from any part of the system. The degree is unique to the student concerned and does not exist as a pre-existing pathway, however flexible. It is important however, not to let the critics of such awards perceive them as some kind of lower status 'pick and mix' programme. Whilst it is possible to devise negotiated systems which have no rules and are completely open for the student to accumulate credit from anywhere in the system, we know of no such courses in the UK. Negotiated awards are bounded by rules which are designed to maintain the standards of the degree and to adhere to many of the conventions of UK academe. The difference, as we shall see later, is that the onus is put upon the student to provide a rationale for the selected choice of modules within the framework of the institutional rules laid down. The ultimate in flexibility comes in the form of programmes of study that have no defining characteristics in terms of content.

Here the student is free, subject to any regulations that the university might specify for any particular reason, to chose modules not from one or two or even three subject areas but from across the whole of the university's provision. By combining all the modules that the student selects, a unique bespoke course is developed.

*Figure 2.7: BA (Hons) negotiated title*

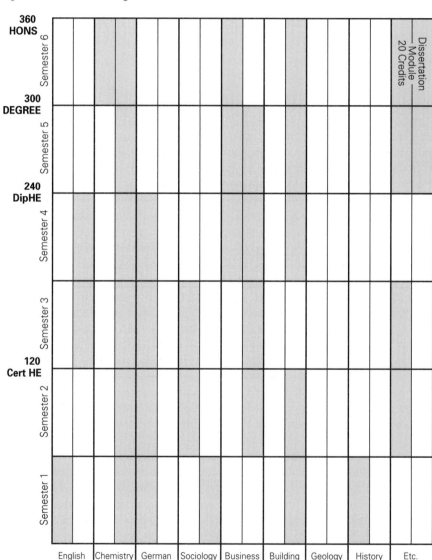

THE NEGOTIATED FIELD IS MADE UP FROM ALL MODULES FROM ALL SETS,
FROM WHICH THE STUDENT SELECTS

Flexibility is often restricted to a scale that can be comfortably handled by small units within the university. This often means at the level of the faculty. Increasing choice through flexibility need not be restricted to schemes within faculties, however. University wide schemes are becoming more common and represent almost the ultimate in CBMS flexibility. They also represent almost the ultimate in complexity because not only do the institutional factors have to be put in place to support choice across a large organization, but academics from very different disciplines need to agree about certain basic issues such as the title of the award.

### Organizing Flexibility

Thus as we move along the continuum of flexibility, it can be seen how, ironically, flexibility requires greater standardization, consistency of policy and regulation. Movement across subject disciplines in this way requires common timetabling processes, agreement about module design, rules governing assessment, loading and variety, and regulations governing the boundaries of choice. It is this standardization, in the context of an academic culture which stresses freedom for the tutor (rather than the student), that causes the most uproar. CBMS requires a change of institutional culture and organization.

The complexity of choice and the standardization which facilitates this means that the university must define, at an *institutional* level, the ways of organizing and describing its curriculum, so that both staff and students can cope with the new freedoms that are presented and the regulations that encourage this freedom can be framed. Traditional organizational structures are not well suited to coping with CBMS. The reason for this is that traditionally universities are organized on a subject basis. Thus departments which contain staff also contain students and contain courses. This one to one relationship between staff, students and courses, works very satisfactorily if there is no need for any of the three to step outside the departmental boundary. As soon as an institution develops a curriculum philosophy, such as that underpinning CBMS, which assumes that students will make choices outside the department, then courses no longer belong to a department (as far as students are concerned) and students no longer identify solely with a single department. At the more flexible ends of the CBMS model they may not even identify with a single faculty. Whatever the organizational structures of the university, the boundaries in place for the purposes of managing the organization are likely to produce barriers to flexibility. Institutions developing CBMS must therefore attempt to meet the organizational requirements of staff, including their need for resources, their professional development, their concerns for their subject, its development and their research. At the same time the organization must respond to the needs of a flexible curriculum and student choice.

### Fields and Sets

There are therefore two organizational dimensions that a university needs to describe in order to do this successfully. The first is related to the students' need. This enables the student to make choices of modules within a particular area. In its simplest form, a student might want to choose a number of modules from business and a number from philosophy and, according to the institutional rules on proportions, develop a programme leading to a Major in business and a Minor in philosophy. Of course the regulations will tell the student to choose from these *subjects*. But language is everything and the term 'subject' might limit institutional course developers to traditional subjects areas indeed like business and philosophy. CBMS approaches are likely to be limited in the first instance to the organizational pattern of the university in subject departmental terms. However, if a new term is used, let us call it *Field* (it could be 'Area' or any other term) it encourages the next move in CBMS development (putting together as cognate parts of a programme), modules that might otherwise not have been identified through traditional subjects and department. Thus whilst an institution might have English, history and philosophy departments and may wish to retain English, history and philosophy areas or Fields from which students will select their modules, the use of the term Field encourages inter and multi-disciplinary developments like, for example, Victorian Studies so that a student could develop a single honours in Victorian Studies as a Major or Minor route. Thus, whilst a Field in Victorian Studies may exist as an expression of the organization of the curriculum, a department of Victorian Studies need not. Departments are the expression of the organization of resources including the *staff* in the university, but this need not be coterminous with the curriculum.

Thus, this approach provides a starting point not only for students to transcend traditional departmental barriers but also for staff, who can step outside traditional subject departments and begin to develop innovative programmes. Fields, whether they are designed on a single cognate subject basis or multi-disciplinary basis or both, are at the heart of student choice. For this reason different Fields may contain the same modules. Thus the level 1 module 'Introduction to Victorian England' may appear in the History Field and the Victorian Studies Field. Students registered on these Fields may be taught together by the same tutor at the same time or separately and by different tutors. We begin to see here how there is the potential for resource savings as the development of modules need not be duplicated just because they are in different Fields. Staff from the department of History may teach the module 'Introduction to Victorian Studies' without necessarily owning the Fields to which it belongs. We begin to see here a further issue which causes consternation in the minds of critics of CBMS, the divorce of ownership from delivery.

Fields, which are the student choice dimension in the organizational

Figure 2.8: *The Victorian studies field*

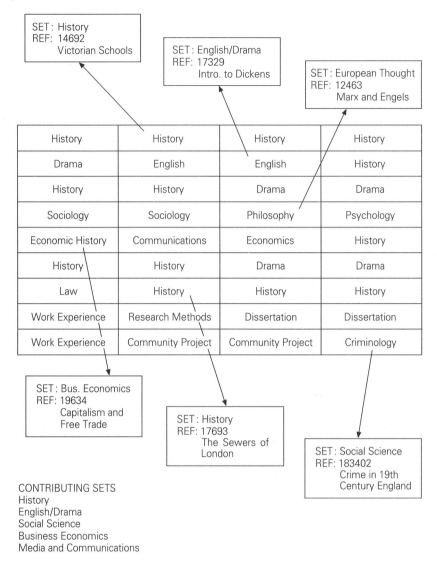

CONTRIBUTING SETS
History
English/Drama
Social Science
Business Economics
Media and Communications

equation, thus contain the regulations governing the selection of modules for students. The dilemmas we spoke of above relating to the ways in which the university must decide on matters of how much credit is necessary in any particular subject for it to count as a single honours programme or as a Major or Minor will be described in *Field Rules*. Ideally such rules will be standard across the whole University and may be something like:

- In order to be a single Honours candidate the student must select at least 240 credits from a Field of which 100 must be at level 3.
- In order to Major in a subject a candidate must select at least 200 credits from a Field of which 100 must be at level 3.
- In order to undertake a Minor in a subject a candidate must select at least 90 credits from a Field of which 30 must be at level 3.

The particular balance would be the outcome of academic debate within the institution. Although a single set of Field rules is desirable, one can envisage the possibility of some Fields standing out as separate. In some professional areas, such as Nursing, one can envisage that not only are modules restricted to students registered on Nursing programmes (no sharing with sociologists!) but also that professional bodies require greater concentration on specialist field modules.

- In order to be a candidate for the degree of BSc (Hons) Nursing a student must undertake 340 credits from the Nursing Field of which at least 120 must be at level 3.

Such arguments that the subject is special and no self respecting graduate can call themselves a graduate in say Business Studies unless they have poked in every nook and cranny of the business studies world is often made when institutional CBMS structures are developed. Some see this as academic conservatism, others as the legitimate protection of subject standards. Either way the debates can be fierce and the compromises frustrating. More often than not the stance taken by professional bodies is quoted to protect a position and quite often on further examination this is a travesty of the real position of the professional body if they have one at all!

If Fields are the basis of student choice it must be recognized that *within* a Field different patterns can emerge. Two students taking the Sociology Field may take some modules in common (especially if they are compulsory), but select a different pattern of modules within the Field rules. Each student therefore has potentially a unique *Pathway* through the Field. Even single Honours students may vary in their module choices. Others taking Major/ Major combinations or Major/Minor combinations will multiply this differentiation as they track different pathways through their Fields. This is an important conceptual leap to make with CBMS programmes. The old concept of *course* becomes tenuous as students develop unique routes through the framework, with potentially as many courses as there are students. This fact and the fact that students no longer necessarily have a departmental 'home' creates significant quality assurance problems for the CBMS institution which can no longer use traditional methods of seeking the views of students on the quality of their course through questionnaires to cohorts. At module level this may be possible but at course (pathway) level it is not, as we shall see in Chapter 7.

There is another dimension to the organization of the CBMS curriculum framework and this relates to the resourcing and quality of the modules. In the same way as students attach themselves to modules, the institution must have a means of resourcing a module both with staff, competent to deliver it, and with accommodation and other materials. It must also have a way of assuring itself of the adequacy of the delivery. This is the institutional side of the equation rather than the student side. In order to operate the system effectively, a university needs to locate the module organizationally in one place in order to organize its resourcing and also its quality management. We will for the sake of argument call this the Module Set. Essentially this is a conceptual box into which all cognate modules are placed. There may be a Set for example for law. This will contain all modules relating to law whether taught as part of the Law Field (for specialist lawyers) or the Building Field (for building students) or Business Field (for business students). Whereas the same law module may appear in a number of Fields it must only appear in one Set. As we shall see later in quality assurance terms this allows comparisons to be made about the way in which that module is being delivered by different staff at different times in different Fields and pathways. It facilitates the fair and equitable assessment of students and the administration of Examination Boards. We will go into more detail in Chapter 7 but essentially if different students are taking the same module in a diverse range of Fields possibly taught by a range of different staff, the institution needs a mechanism to ensure that the standard of assessment (both from the point of view of the student and the tutor) is appropriate. If assessment were based upon Fields alone, then the Introduction to Law module taught by the lawyers from the department of Law to LLB students might be of a different standard from that taught by the builders from the department of Building to building students, despite the fact they have the same learning outcomes and levels. It is important that we do not muddle this with the question of module content. We would expect, even with the same module outcomes, the builders to put a different spin on the content which is delivered to building students in order to achieve the learning outcomes. We would not expect this to mean that the standard of this level 1 module is lower (or higher) for building students. This would be grossly unfair. Sets become a mechanism to ensure that all modules in a cognate area, no matter where they are taught, by whom, to whom, achieve the same standard of recruitment, resourcing and outcome. The relationship of modules to Fields and Sets can be illustrated in Figure 2.9.

The main resource for a module is the staff who teach it. It could be argued that Sets could be coterminous with departments in which staff reside for their pay and rations and academic succour. Indeed in some cases this might be possible, especially where there is a close link between the subject department, the focus of the Set and where the modules within the Set are tightly controlled to restrict access. Thus a Nursing Field which contains pathways leading to the BSc(Hons) Nursing and the BSc(Hons) Nursing Practice

*Figure 2.9: The relationship of modules to fields and sets*

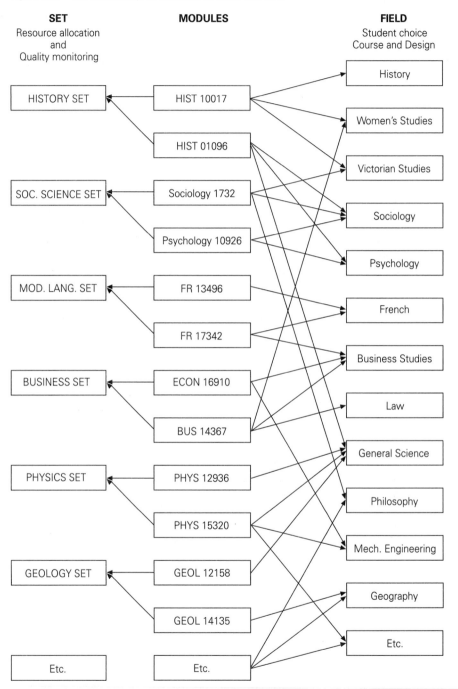

| SET | MODULES | FIELD |
| --- | --- | --- |
| Resource allocation and Quality monitoring | | Student choice Course and Design |

- HISTORY SET
- SOC. SCIENCE SET
- MOD. LANG. SET
- BUSINESS SET
- PHYSICS SET
- GEOLOGY SET
- Etc.

- HIST 10017
- HIST 01096
- Sociology 1732
- Psychology 10926
- FR 13496
- FR 17342
- ECON 16910
- BUS 14367
- PHYS 12936
- PHYS 15320
- GEOL 12158
- GEOL 14135
- Etc.

- History
- Women's Studies
- Victorian Studies
- Sociology
- Psychology
- French
- Business Studies
- Law
- General Science
- Philosophy
- Mech. Engineering
- Geography
- Etc.

might be restricted entirely to professional nurses. All Nursing Modules may be in the Nursing Set. All modules may be taught by staff from the department of Nursing and there is a one to one alignment. These cases are rare and indeed if the CBMS developers set out to achieve such alignment they would be building into their system the kinds of constraints and inflexibilities that are anathema to CBMS. More likely is that any particular module in, say the Politics Set could be taught by staff from the department of Sociology (in the Sociology Field), the department of Politics (in the Victorian Studies Field and the Politics Field) and the department of Philosophy (in the Ethics Field). The Set mechanism is designed to coordinate such offerings and attempt to produce common standards. Some have argued that it makes sense to organize departments around Sets if it is not possible to organize Sets around departments. In other words put everybody who teaches law whether in the department of Law, Building or Philosophy, into one department where they can talk law together and be used flexibly around the institution delivering modules to students in the various Fields. Law would therefore be a Set and a department. This attractive solution has its drawbacks. Firstly it calls forth a massive organizational change where members of staff are removed from one department and put organizationally and sometimes physically into another department. Thus the law expert in the department of Building who has taught law to builders for many years is suddenly removed and surrounded by lawyers rather than builders. This may have benefits, but the building Field Leader may see this as the thin end of the wedge if one day the department of Law furnishes him or her with a lawyer to teach 'Introduction to Law' to building students who is insufficiently submerged in the language and culture of building! But this is a moot point and some organizations have based themselves on this 'servicing' philosophy. A more fundamental criticism of this department/Set alignment is that it builds a rigidity into the CBMS which is counter productive. The whole point of divorcing the curriculum organization from the university organization is that the curriculum organization can be changed quickly with new Sets, Fields and modules being developed and disbanded as new markets are identified, and new subject disciplines created. University organizations are very slow to change, affecting as they do people's roles, status and job satisfaction.

Thus CBMS frameworks require the dual axes of *student-choice organization*, which we have chosen to call the Field, and *module-management organization*, which we have chosen to call the Set. In parallel to this the university must organize its departmental structures to look after the legitimate needs of the staff. The danger is that in so doing the university creates an unworkable matrix in which staff belong to a department, possibly coordinate a Set but certainly teach modules in a Set, possibly lead a Field in which modules from various Sets reside and certainly teach on modules in Fields and Sets! The potential for muddle and confusion are rife! This is a major dilemma for the designers of CBMS. It requires a radical review of existing ways of looking at the university and an attempt to align a curriculum delivery model, which stresses flexibility and the breakdown of barriers with organizational structures, which by definition reinforce barriers. If the worst elements of matrices are to be avoided (namely staff have more than one master) then the circle needs to be squared. This can be achieved by implementing an approach that requires the curriculum to be managed *collectively* rather than, as is traditional, by separate and often powerful heads of departments or deans of faculty. In this sense the effective management of CBMS strengthens the corporate ethos of an institution and undermines more diffuse processes of management. Equally the full potential of CBMS will not be realized if such cooperation fails to materialize.

# Chapter 3

# **Modules and Credit**

Credit-based systems do not have to be modular but many are. Classical modularism insofar as it relates to credit accumulation, comes in a number of forms. In its most pure form it provides a single standard framework which is embedded right across the institution. Whatever the academic discipline concerned, deviation from the standard is carefully controlled. In this classical form modules will be the same size measured in notional hours; they will be delivered within a common time frame, usually either a semester or term; they will be assessed within the time frame of the module itself and on the basis of common principles relating to assessment criteria, grades and regulations. Since, under this classical model, students have potential access to modules from different parts of the university and can in principle mix different subject elements (sociology with English), the differences between the diverse academic and operational cultures, so often implicit in university life, soon become exposed. This is one of the real dilemmas of modularity and credit. The many untested presuppositions of academics in their everyday professional lives that have been subterranean for centuries are brought to the surface in CBMS and challenged, not by students but by academics in other disciplines who hold different taken for granted suppositions about the nature of the HE world. We would argue that this is a welcome, but long overdue, development and should not be seen as a criticism of CBMS.

There are many variants to the classical form which result from individual institutions attempting to tackle key dilemmas which face them when they seek to go modular. We can see this in the first of our module issues. How do we determine module size?

## **Module Size**

Even if we agree the standard credit rating of modules (which we discuss below) we need to articulate that against the number of hours that students will devote to that module. In other words when we agree a module will be say 10 credits, how is that to translate itself into delivery at the chalk face? Most modular systems make a distinction between 'tutor contact' and 'student committed time' or 'learning time' (Theodossin, 1986, p. 13). In other words it is recognized that the effort a student is expected to put into a module is usually greater than the amount of time that a tutor will have in face to face contact with that student. The total learning time may be say 100 hours, of which 100 are committed by the student and within which only 10 hours are devoted to tutor contact. We can envisage some modules that require no direct tutor input at all because they are by distance learning and others that have a significant amount of tutor input because of the more didactic methods that are deemed necessary. The dilemma however, is to agree *across the institution* what the standard student committed time ought to be. Without such agreement, module sizes or shapes will be different (despite common credit ratings) and thus practices such as common timetabling to facilitate greater flexibility in the design of a student's programme will be rendered impossible. Committed time is usually referred to as *notional* time in recognition that some students work well above the norm whilst others work well below it! The need to establish a norm illustrates the transparency that CBMS introduces. Often issues of student committed time are conveniently ignored in traditional systems.

This approach reverses the once normal 'finger in the wind' method. Rather than developing the curriculum on the basis of how many lectures and seminars the tutor feels it is necessary to have in order 'to cover the ground', the ground to be covered needs to be fenced in according to the amount of committed time that is dictated by the institution's agreed framework system. The key question then is how many hours are available for the standard module? Modular systems require academics to be much more precise about such matters. It is not a question of saying, 'we are going to cover these topics over the next 10 weeks', as might have been said in the past, and still is in some traditionally based institutions, but of saying, 'this module is worth 100 committed hours or 75 committed hours or whatever so what content can I, as tutor, develop in this time period, and what might be the appropriate learning outcomes for students?'

For many years such questions were not asked, let alone answered. Where courses were not modular, but stretched across a number of terms, students knew that the course had a beginning and an end and they had an attendance timetable. However, when courses are modularized they are given a value or worth made explicit in the form of a credit rating. The credit is merely a means of exchange. However, if modular systems make matters more transparent they become more transparent for students, they also become more transparent to 'politicians' worried about students and staff not working sufficiently hard, managers wishing to increase 'productivity' and fee-payers wishing to get value for money. When an institution decides to adopt a truly modular system, the institutional debate is often fearsome, since different academic disciplines have different histories and traditions regarding content, delivery and pacing. Few wish to compromise. How much more so should any national debate be if a common framework is to be introduced! If the debate is not fearsome then it is being carefully managed and manipulated. In practice CBMS institutions have approached the issue of module size in the following way. A normal working week is notionally 40 hours and this should be true for students as well.

Therefore a student over a 30 week teaching year should do 1200 hours of study. Since a year is 120 credits (see below) then one credit is 10 hours.

40 hours × 30 weeks = 1200 hours per year

$$\frac{1200 \text{ hours}}{120 \text{ credits}} = 10 \text{ hours per credit}$$

Thus a 10-credit module is 100 hours and a 20 is 200 hours. This seems very reasonable and straightforward if somewhat neat. However it creates further dilemmas, especially for those institutions which have a significant number of part-time students and employed students who operate on a part-time basis. The argument goes that building the module size around full-time student assumptions of a 40 hour week over 30 weeks, neglects that part-time students are often also practitioners in their field of study and are therefore involved in a very real way in the subject. To expect them to undertake modules whose size is based on the assumption of a divorce from work is unrealistic. Teachers on in-service BEd degrees, nurses enhancing skills and knowledge, unqualified accountants studying for professional recognition are all developing the content of their 'academic' study out of their everyday practice, and relating their class-based theory back into the work place. Such vocational courses are becoming more common. They would argue on this basis for a reduction in the notional committed time *in lieu* of the very real contribution that work makes to their study. Far better, they argue, to reduce the committed time in recognition of the fact that the world of work offers a complementary learning environment for those students who are undertaking vocationally relevant degrees. However, there is a further dilemma. Even those who advocate such an approach on philosophical or practical grounds recognize that the argument does not hold true in all cases. Whilst the 'alternative learning environment' argument might be pertinent for the building-site foreman seeking to gain a degree in building or the unqualified practising social worker seeking a social work degree, it does not hold true for the local supermarket check-out assistant working towards a degree in history! Proponents of the alternative learning environment argument counter by arguing that mature part-time students are more competent than fresh from school students who do not have the directly relevant work experience or transferable skills that maturity and work provide. This 'mature students have transferable skills' argument will become more important as the UK HE system starts to identify more explicitly than it has hitherto what these transferable skills are. More significant is the developing concern for graduate skills, or graduateness, in which there is the beginnings of the identification of what non subject specific qualities we expect from graduating students (Dearing, 1997; HEQC, 1995b). These academic arguments are often reinforced by resource managers. For them it is better for the notional committed time to be 75 hours for a 10-credit module. With 100 hours it is difficult to timetable more than one module in say one evening, and this therefore increases the need to lengthen the part-time experience or weekly burden of attendance. Indeed why make the assumption that the working week is normally 40 hours in any case? Why not 30, or 35? Similarly there is no standard academic year of 30 weeks. For some it is much less and for others much more.

Such disparities make the establishment of a national framework extremely problematic. Different institutions have different pedagogic structures and different profiles of students who have different needs. Of course it would be possible at a national level to let a thousand blossoms bloom. But the implications of this is to make explicit something that has been quietly forgotten for a long time and has remained unexposed until more transparent CBMS systems required answers. Degrees from different institutions are very different in terms of the formal burden they place upon students. There must be many philosophy degrees that are based upon 1200 hours per year notional committed time and many upon much less than this. They would all claim however to provide the student with the necessary graduate qualities expected of a philosophy graduate. A national system can live with this amount of variability as long as not too many probing questions are asked. This also relates to credit transfer. Provided a receiving institution does not feel inclined to note the actual hour assumptions behind the credits gained by a student from elsewhere, business can continue. Turning a blind eye has been an important principle in HE to date. However, *within* an institution, it is vitally important to chose a common hourage and stick to it. If within the same institution some modules within the same framework are clearly different, then the possibility of flexibility of curriculum design for staff and students alike is seriously undermined. If the same module is to be used for example for full-time conventional and part-time in-service students then the basis of the delivery must be agreed. This is even more true if the students are on occasion to be taught side by side. Modular systems do in theory provide economies but only if curriculum flexibility is increased, ironically by reducing diversity.

## Module Volume

One of the crucial issues that must be considered in developing a credit-based programme of studies is the number of credits to be allocated to any particular award. If we take the three year full-time honours degree as our starting point (as most UK CATS systems do) and then articulate other awards against it, then we must first determine how many credits will be gained in relation to this award. In other words how many credits is the undergraduate degree worth. This can of course be any number and can be converted to any other number if it is to be articulated against other degrees in other institutions. Most institutions in the UK have adopted 360 credits as the norm for the three year degree. So let us for the time being adopt this figure in order to illustrate some of the issues that arise.

The first issue is whether the number of credits relates to the status of the award or the length of time the award is *designed* to take (not how long it might take an individual student). A three year honours degree worth 360 credits is often broken down into its constituent parts thus:

Year 1   120 credits                    to Certificate in HE
Year 2   120 credits   *in addition*   to Diploma in HE
Year 3   120 credits   *in addition*   to Honours Degree

What then do you do about degree programmes that are *by design* longer than the UK norm for a first degree? Is the BEd (Hons), which because of the practice-based elements was four years long, still worth 360 credits like everybody else's degree or 480 credits? Similar issues arise in the area of languages which include overseas placements and also engineering first degrees (sometimes called MEng), for which it is argued that students need four years to complete the content. Is the undergraduate MEng, which is a first degree but four years in length, worth 360 or 480? There are no right answers only consequences!

The 'equal credit for equal work' philosophy suggests that it is only fair that a student who does more work (in this case 33 per cent more) ought to achieve more credit. Each credit is worth precisely the same as other credits in terms of the notional committed time appertaining to it (see above). *Thus what is equal here is the value of the credit. What is unequal is the value of the award.* An alternative approach is to treat all awards the same (360 credits) and spread the credits across the time period. This means, of course, that the student on the BEd(Hons) does more committed time in order to gain one credit compared with a colleague say on the English degree. All degrees whatever their planned length will be 360 credits. This approach is more in line with a traditional UK philosophy that all degrees achieve the same standards and the same 'graduateness' outcomes. It is therefore anathema to give greater credit for one rather than another. We must be careful with this argument since there is a danger of associating credit with some concept of assessment level. That is a different issue. Nevertheless this is a point. Unless you agree to a standard number for every degree, you are admitting that some credits somehow have more or less value than others or there are different *types* of credit. If these courses were discrete or isolated it would not matter in the least that one was 480 credits and another 360, or both were 360 but one was four years and another was three. However, credit systems are designed to facilitate transfer and flexible course design. Students sometimes wish to transfer out of their programmes onto other (more appropriate) courses or indeed into other institutions. In pre credit-based systems a 'weak' student on a BEd might have had to remain on the programme and fail or become a poor or unmotivated teacher, or drop out of higher education altogether. Course designers were unlikely to be able to teach BA(English) students alongside BEd(Secondary School English) students on the same module. We therefore have a volume dilemma. If the four year degree is rated at 360, then when students seek transfer at the end of say Year One they have available for negotiation only 90 credits (360 ÷ 4) compared to the student transferring the other way who has 120. (This ignores the important distinction between general and specific credits which is taken up in Chapter 6.) In addition, since under this methodology the student does as much work but the content is worth less it is impossible to design programmes that integrate BEd students with say English students and therefore gain flexibility, resource savings, and other benefits that might accrue from common teaching.

In subject areas such as nursing, teaching, languages and other four year programmes which contain the equivalent of practice or work-based elements, course teams have attempted to avoid the dilemma by attempting to remove some of the credits from the calculation altogether. They do this by making a distinction between the practice-based elements, for which the student gains up to say 120 (let us call them P) credits, and the rest is 'proper' academic work for which they gain *academic* credits. This allows the one to one exchange of academic credits across the system, with the P credits put to one side. A 480 credit four year programme becomes 360 academic credits and 120 P credits. Thus the course is in one sense 360 credits and in another 480. This might still mean that after the first year the BEd student only has 90 credits because the other 30 are P credits. However, at least the credits transferred are exactly the same in volume terms, and the student has no less a chance of transfer than say the historian into the sociology degree where only some academic credits will be directly transferable. It also means that course designers can base the size of their modules on a single institutional standard, no matter what the degree, thus allowing flexibility and resource savings. But of course this P device has its limitations. Many course designers who develop practice-based degrees argue that theory and practice are so interlinked that you should not (even if you could) divide the so called academic modules from the practice. They are all one. This argument is often put by nurse educators. The second problem is that the P device is not open to courses that have no practice base but are genuinely longer because they need more content. Most institutions have chosen to differentiate three year from four year degrees by giving the latter 480 credits rather than choosing to treat each as the same with the standard 360 credits. The 480 credit solution and the philosophy behind it is the one that has therefore found the most favour despite the dilemmas that lead on from it. It means that credit transfer requires very careful analysis, because you cannot take at face value the number of credits a student might be transferring from such programmes. When a conventional student has 240 credits they are two-thirds through a degree. When a 480 student has 240 credits they are only half way through.

This is nothing new of course. The problems become even more complex if we take an international view. Overseas degrees, even where considered equivalent in standing to the UK degree, are often by design taught over a longer period of time. How then do you facilitate transfer on an international basis? Since such transfer may be for short periods of exchange, where students travel overseas for a term or semester or two, matching experience becomes very complex and the advantage of the credit system as a facilitator of smooth transfer becomes problematic. Of course, nearer to home, the articulation between the Scottish degree based on four years as the norm and the English degree of three illustrates the dilemma admirably. Having said that differentiation (having both a 480 and 360 credit norm) has found favour, it must be noted that this principle is applied to different types of degree, not to different types of student. In other words once all these dilemmas have been resolved we have to apply the resolution to any mode of degree delivery. Thus part-time students on a sociology degree take longer than those on the full-time degree. The time they take depends on the speed at which they build up the credits and the credit rating of the modules taken, not on the length of time it takes the student. Thus the part-time sociology degree is still rated at 360 credits despite the fact that the part-time norm for attendance might require six years. The part-time student does not need 720 credits or we open up all the problems again and it is part-time students that most often avail themselves of all the advantages of credit transfer! Equally as proposals are put in place for newer accelerated degrees (HEFCE, 1996), the requirement remains to gain the 360 credits despite the fact the course may be two calendar years rather than the normal three academic. It is the student who accelerates the pace of study. The degree remains the same.

The number or volume of modules that a conventional student is expected to take in any one full-time academic year is a matter of choice for course designers. Conventionally the number of credits across the year is divided by the number of modules chosen. Thus if we have resolved our earlier dilemmas and selected 120 credits as the basis of our calculation for a full-time year then any number that divides into 120 seems a reasonable choice. Thus modules could be

    5   Credits in which case 24 modules are required to fill the full-time year.

   10   Credits in which case 12 modules are required to fill the full-time year.

   15   Credits in which case 8 modules are required to fill the full-time year.

   20   Credits in which case 6 modules are required to fill the full-time year.

How do we resolve this dilemma? Again there are no right answers. The first thing is to recognize that, in a modular system, the smaller the number of credits per module, the greater the number of modules. If you are looking to maximize flexibility, small modules are best since you can make small modifications to a programme and make use of a greater number of modules with the least disruption to the core. On the other hand the more modules a student takes, the more assessment is required in order to demonstrate that the outcomes of the discrete modules have been attained. Ironically, in systems that are non-modular or where modules are very large it is generally recognized, but seldom acknowledged, that assessment rarely covers all the outcomes or objectives. Not only is the burden of assessment greater on the student where small modules exist but the burden of marking increases (Billing, 1996, p. 16).

It is therefore a question of balance, but one that cannot be divorced from the structure of the academic year. If the year is divided into two semesters then any of the above patterns are feasible. 60 credits will be the standard delivery in each semester divided into 12, 6, 4 or 3 modules per semester. On a termly basis then the 15 credit module will not work since 40 credits have to be delivered in any term. Some institutions are considering a fourth term. Here the standard of a 20 credit module will not work since the norm will be 30 credits per term.

Some staff who have struggled in their institutions to develop 'classical' modular systems where a single framework determines all aspects of provision become frustrated when confronted by institutions that claim to be modular but have instead opted for 'soft modularity'. Soft modularity is nothing more than the process of placing boundaries around elements of content, irrespective of the amount of time devoted to those particular areas or the assessment related to them. This being the case, the size of the modules that have been created will vary. The next step in credit terms is to give a credit rating to each chunk. The number of credits will relate to the size of the chunk. Thus the first year of a course might look like Figure 3.1.

*Figure 3.1: Illustration of the first year of a soft modular course*

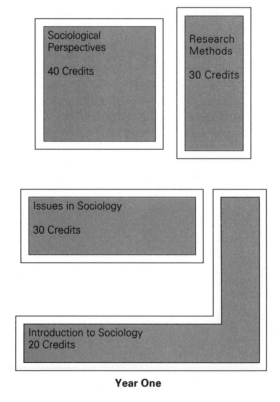

**Year One**

Here the content adds up to the required 120 credits but the size and shape of the modules are variable, and possibly cut across terms or semesters. In contrast a classic modular system might look something like Figure 3.2, where the size of the modules has been standardized and content redesigned to meet the framework that has been put in place.

*Figure 3.2: Illustration of a classic modular system*

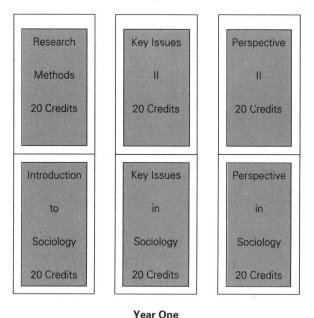

**Year One**

The advantage of the soft modular approach is that it is easy to introduce since it challenges very little. It can therefore be used as a first developmental step along the road to a more classical form of modularism. It is a way of introducing modular and credit concepts without the unwary noticing too much. However, it has little to commend it since it provides few if any of the real benefits of modular and credit-based programmes. Since modules are different shapes and sizes, the possibility of transfer between programmes in the same institution or between institutions is extremely problematic and is probably limited to key stages in a programme, usually the end of year. (Many, of course, will see advantage in locking the student, and therefore the funding, into the institution or even department by making transfer problematic.) There are also internal disadvantages, however. Despite the language of flexibility that soft modularity utilizes, the reality is that all programmes across the institution are so diverse that the possibility of sharing modules is seriously undermined. Timetabling on a common basis is a nightmare. There can therefore be few economies of scale for resource managers. For the student there is less real, or no, choice. Whilst in theory they can build up a credit-based programme, in reality their ability to select modules from non-cognate areas (or even from related areas outside the norm) is seriously reduced by the difficulties in making the credits add up to the appropriate numbers let alone finding the fit in timetables. In the long run, soft modularism is an ideal device for not modularizing and for not basing programmes on a credit accumulation system, but appearing to do so!

However, as a first step towards classical modularism it is helpful since it does introduce the often contentious issue of assessing students at the end of the chunk of work rather than leaving the assessment to the end of year examinations. It begins to introduce many of the dilemmas that the HE world has for so long avoided by being able to avoid each other! Real dialogue between academic traditions within higher education has been rare. If Fine Artists and Engineers do not need to agree about that which they must have in common they have no need to engage in debate at all. CBMS requires dialogue between academic groups with their differing cultures. It still remains acceptable to some to retain different assessment traditions, classification methodologies, regulations on mitigation and compensation, the meaning of graduateness, despite the hidden inequalities this produces for students. The climate is changing, however, and CBMS has been the prime mover in bringing to the top of the academic agenda the problematic nature of many subject-based conventional wisdoms.

Classical forms of modularity also challenge deep seated traditions of another kind. The first is that they challenge notions of academic autonomy. Academic staff are no longer at liberty to determine those aspects of delivery and content that had previously been within their sole domain. The number of hours available for the topic becomes a more critical factor in determining that content than previously. The preciseness of the expected learning outcomes or objectives becomes a matter for public scrutiny as does the nature and timing of the assessment and the regime behind that assessment. The form of marking (grade, literal or numerical, criteria and level) all become externally imposed. For managers the balance shifts towards greater centralization, since standardization is required in terms of, for example, timetabling and other working practices. We must be highly suspicious, therefore, when national bodies or regional consortia claim consensus or even majority agreement over many of the issues discussed here. Consensus is likely to be false or forced.

## Module Levels

All degree programmes claim to maintain certain standards. In the past the definition of these standards has been somewhat vague, and it is only recently that through the 'graduateness' research (HEQC, 1997b) attempts are being made to develop an objective, or at least stand alone, definition of what constitutes the standard to be reached by the end of the degree programme. The

Quality Assurance Agency (QAA) has started research on this issue and selected the areas of law, chemistry and history as the first degree programmes to be focused upon with a view to defining common standards. The CBMS curriculum has been the culprit in raising issues which have remained hidden for many years. To date much to do with standards has been implicit or part of the academic's secret garden. But even the founding fathers (and mothers) of the credit-based modular curriculum were content to fudge some very significant issues in their attempt to move matters along in a hostile environment. If QAA is to make a real and immediate impact on standard issues it should choose not single subject areas with well worn standards pathways and close supervision by external professional bodies but the complexities that arise from combined programmes and multi-disciplinary approaches made possible through a modularized curriculum.

The key dilemma regarding *level* is what should the number and nature of the levels be in an undergraduate programme of study? In many modular systems, level has often been defined by reference to that good old stand-by, the length of the degree. The argument goes something like this. Modules undertaken in the first year of study of a full-time degree are expected to be at the level of what one expects the full-time student to be able to achieve in the first year! This somewhat circular argument, which requires no explicit definition of what we, the academic community, expect by the end of the first year, is extended to the second and third years. Thus many modular systems have three undergraduate levels. The issue of the number of levels to which modules might be allocated in order to indicate progression and standard has been complicated by the issue raised in the Introduction, namely the development of CBMS on top of a traditional time-based UK system, rather than on a truly innovative model from first principles. The issue of level needs to be considered in the context of the need for CBMS to be underpinned by greater transparency. Traditional UK models of degrees have been rather coy about expressing outcomes, and levels of those outcomes, in an explicit way. Much has been shrouded in the mysteries of the Examination Board and the 'professional' and often secret judgments of the examiners (both internal and external). Somewhat inexplicably in view of the work already done in the UK on credit frameworks, Dearing establishes a new framework (Dearing, 1997). He establishes an undergraduate framework with four levels (with virtually no appreciation of the notion of outcomes) which are related to stages of progression:

| | |
|---|---|
| Certificate | level H1 |
| Diploma | level H2 |
| Degree | level H3 |
| Honours degree | level H4 |

This sounds very logical and appears to adhere to the principles of accumulating credit in a progressive fashion at different levels until an honours degree is achieved. However, whilst espousing the virtues of credit in the achievement of learning (p. 152) he fails to understand the basic principles of the credit accumulation model (as we show in Chapter 9). It is possible that Dearing takes the approach that he does in order to present a framework which appears to be successful in holding together a genuine UK-based approach, which can cope with the Scottish four year degree and the English three year programme. Many of the existing credit-based and modular degrees within the English system are based upon an application of the principles of the traditional three year full-time degree to CBMS. This was the direction taken by the CNAA in establishing its framework in the late 1980s (CNAA, 1989). The model adopted is as follows:

Year 1   Modules are at Level 1
Year 2   Modules are at Level 2
Year 3   Modules are at Level 3

The advantage of this model (unlike Dearing) is that it does not do too much violence to the existing (although often unstated) principle, that Year 3 is higher than Year 1. This is therefore much easier to introduce without causing too much consternation amongst academic colleagues, including external examiners and members of external quality bodies. It also has the advantage of being simple to understand for staff and students alike. This was certainly an important model, especially in the early days of CBMS where enthusiasts sought to persuade colleagues that the system could work alongside the traditional linear time-based model of a degree beloved of many in the UK. However, this model does create some important dilemmas, many of which have been ignored or avoided in the national and regional consortia debates in an attempt to produce some consensus about a single CBMS framework. This three level solution, despite its attractiveness, is a structural answer to what is perceived to be a structural issue. However, a minority of CBMS institutions have sought to respond to the levels' issues by approaching the dilemma through the curriculum and its assessment, which we believe to be more appropriate. The whole point of CBMS is to recognize and build in, as an integral part of the degree programme, the notion of flexibility. One key aspect of flexibility is that students may not necessarily be spending only three years of their time on degree study on a full-time basis through phased periods of study. Many students will now wish to study part-time or on an extended full-time basis. But even if we assume no increase in the number of such students, the reality has always been that there will be part-time programmes which last longer than three years. In other words a course may well be five or six years in planned length for part-time study. The proponents of three levels based on sequential full-time years need therefore not only to map their three levels to the reality of four, five or six years study but also argue convincingly that a mature student in, say, year 4 is no different from a 19-year-old full-time student in year 2. This was simple in the early days of CBMS where the niceties of explicit outcomes and attainment were largely ignored in the academic community. The position is now made more complex by the introduction, through funded provision, of accelerated two calendar year programmes which undermine many of the reasoned arguments of the three level advocates. The Accelerated and Intensive Routes (AIRs) Study argued that the 10 pilot courses funded by HEFCE had been successful in many ways. Significantly many of the participants in the project:

> planned to re-deploy their AIRs provision by developing flexibility in other ways, including more part-time options within their modular schemes. Such plans were in line with the External Examiner view that special AIRs programmes were unnecessary, as in a good modular scheme 'it should be an option for students to accumulate credits at a rate which suits them'. (HEFCE, 1996, p. 23)

The new requirement to be much more open and explicit about assessment and outcomes has now made it much more apparent than hitherto that the more gradations you have in the system the more refined the criteria have to be for differentiating them. Tutors assessing work are now required to go beyond 'this piece of work or that has a B+ or B++ feel about it'. They are expected to ensure that it fulfils the explicit outcomes at a specifically defined level which the student knows openly and is prepared to challenge if necessary. Not only do staff need to be able therefore to make the fine judgments which distinguish level 1 from level 2 and level 2 from level 3, let alone Dearing's 1, 2, 3 and 4 (Dearing, 1997), but they need to do this when level 1 is being taught to second year students on a part-time programme. As important, students have to understand these fine distinctions. This is not to say this cannot be done, and many would argue they are doing it. It might however, be difficult to demonstrate convincingly and unambiguously that it is being done with validity and reliability. Fortunately much can still be hidden in the secrecy of the assessment processes. The difficulty of making fine and precise judgments has led some to retain a model which is based more upon the perspective adopted by some of the older universities, namely the concept of the Part 1 stage and the 'Final' stage, where the judgments are much broader and there is less pretence at sophistication. This principle is adopted and then adapted to underpin the requirements of a more open system of assessment and more explicit curriculum model based on transparent outcomes. Thus the tutor is confronted with a less sophisticated task in attempting to pitch the delivery of his or her course on *King Lear* at an appropriate level. Rather than the question being, 'is this level 2 module sufficiently academic not to be level 1 and not so sophisticated as to be level 3?' it becomes, 'is this a foundation module or an "advanced" module?'. The tutor does not need to worry whether this is a third year part-timer or second year full-timer. Indeed it is possible that the groups could be mixed. Thus levels may be described as:

Basic or Foundation, Level B/F
Higher or Honours, Level H

Proponents of this model state that it has other advantages. In structural terms it is advantageous to resource managers and timetablers and those curriculum managers who wish to develop truly flexible patterns of delivery without practical concerns regarding timetabling inhibiting them. Put succinctly, the more levels you have the greater number of timetabling variables you have and therefore the more slots required. As numbers increase and pressure on resources becomes greater, then matching student needs with staff time becomes paramount. As the curriculum becomes more explicit, then universities will need to deliver precisely what they claim to do. If they claim delivery is at three levels, then it must be seen to be. The mixing of cohorts will for them be more problematic. The problem with this two level approach is that it exposes more explicitly than the three level approach (although the issue is still there) the traditionally unstated *progression principle*. It thus becomes more difficult to introduce convincingly to colleagues and more difficult to convince external bodies rooted in more traditional conventional wisdoms as to its merits. The unstated progression principle is that progression is always time-based and that by definition what a student does in year three or four is by outcome, and must be by design, somehow higher or better or more important or sophisticated than work undertaken in year two or three. This is the linear view of progression. This view assumes continual and therefore infinite progression that peaks in the final year of study. Advocates of the two level system would argue that there are in fact very few subjects that are truly linear and many that would make the claim are probably less linear than they would suggest. The obvious candidates are mathematics, sciences and engineering. What may be linear is the knowledge which is transmitted as part of the building block of the curriculum. This becomes a timetabling issue to ensure that $X$ comes before $Y$. You cannot do fractions until you have learnt to divide.

Progression in terms of level, rather than knowledge-flow (or the grasp of complex concepts), requires an explicit demonstration of expectations and the advocates of two levels claim to be more 'honest' in the identification of outcomes at an explicitly defined level than those who go for more sophisticated (multi-level) models and those who have avoided the debate altogether. It is interesting to note that designers of CBMS postgraduate courses have almost uniformly accepted one level (4 or M) across postgraduate programmes, whether full-time, part-time, work-focused or theoretical. Can it be assumed therefore that the critics of two levels, in undergraduate programmes, believe that no progression exists during postgraduate study? Are all postgraduate courses designed for students to hit the track already running and keep to the same speed throughout? Many postgraduate course designers would point to the importance of the dissertation as the culmination of the programme. In the same way two level CBMS designers would argue that they facilitate progression in terms of adding sophistication to the students' understanding through the curriculum itself, through special modules which integrate concepts and themes, and through dissertations which require sophisticated application of ideas.

If CBMS is about curriculum flexibility then advocates of the two level model would claim that the single differentiation of level allows for earlier decision making, if the student so wishes, in terms of programmes to be followed within course regulations. Students and course designers have only two levels of regulations to chart their way through, compared with three levels, with all the impediments on free choice that regulations may impose. Advocates of the two level model would also argue that their lack of differentiation (or sophistication) in levels is an advantage in assessing individual claims for the Accreditation of Prior Experiential Learning (APEL) and Accreditation of Prior Learning (APL) (see Chapter 6). In both APL and APEL staff are being asked to make judgments about other people's courses or students' uncertificated learning and then grade those experiences. Again the degree of sophistication implied in these processes is immense and, whilst recognized, conveniently overlooked. To be able to differentiate this experience as being made up of bits of acquired learning which is in part at level 2 and in part at level 3 or all squashed in between level 1 and level 3 represents an achievement which is impressive and one suspects unfulfilled in reality. On the other hand the two level approach is, critics would argue, somewhat blunt. Advocates would counter that our current understanding of reliable and valid processes of APL/APEL are such that blunt is honest, and what is more, better understood by the students who are the subject of the processes. Students are also better able to judge the fairness of the APL/APEL rating more easily. This approach also allows for the process of claiming APL/APEL credit to be student driven rather than tutor determined.

## Module Learning Outcomes

It is a strange irony that in education we are so resistant to, and suspicious of, change. In circumstances other than when the change relates to ourselves and our practice we would probably agree that change is synonymous with learning and development. We are particularly fond of describing developments in teaching and learning as 'old wine in new bottles'. It does us no credit to stretch this metaphor too far. The move towards using learning outcomes as the key descriptors of learning 'content' has, in general, been a development that has happened in parallel with the development of credit-based and modular systems. However, the learning outcomes approach has not been adopted across the sector by all CBMS institutions and even within institutions the understanding and implementation of the approach has been incomplete and patchy. Thus in an HEQC study (HEQC, 1996a, p. 19) only half of the sampled institutions had developed, or were moving towards specifying, learning outcomes and in addition 'the provision of criteria which specify the standard of performance necessary to demonstrate the achievement of learning outcomes . . . is less well developed'. In our view this is because the approach is actually a more radical and far reaching change than we generally take it to be and challenges many of the assumptions on which our historical mind sets are based. Like credit, learning outcomes require subscription to the belief that students are likely to learn most effectively within a transparent system that offers explicit criteria about what they are expected to achieve. This is not the same thing as providing syllabus information about the subject content of a module or course or about providing indicators about what the teachers intend to teach. If we are honest, the general availability, even of this kind of information to students, has not been universal practice. In some dark corners, its relevance may have even been questioned! However, the most common dilemma that institutions will face in adopting learning outcomes is the debate that will ensue concerning the way in which they differ or not from the more commonly used objectives (Allan, 1996).

There are several issues here. The first issue concerns the extent to which the institution is already working to an established system of learning object-ives. The second and most important issue is whether the learning objectives that are worked to are in fact learning or teaching objectives. The difference is crucial. What is clear is that the implications of the difference are not always appreciated or understood. The learning outcomes approach requires us to give explicit details about *learning* as a measurable, assessable *output* that the student will recognize. This is distinct from details about the teaching, and the *input* side of the equation that, although useful in itself, does no more than set out an action plan from the teacher's point of view. If we are genuinely concerned with learning and the way in which this educates and empowers students then the latter is not good enough, at least not on its own. The use of learning outcomes therefore offers a challenge to the traditional power relationship that exists between teachers and students. The 'I teach, you learn' model needs to be modified. It becomes, 'in order that you might achieve the given learning (outcomes) I will teach the following in the following way'. The initial dilemma then is not centred on the distinction between outcomes and objectives but on whether these terms describe learning rather than teaching. Several other dilemmas follow from this. All must be addressed if the out-comes approach is to work. Changing the emphasis from teaching and input to learning and output through an outcomes approach does not undervalue or undermine the importance of teachers or of subject specialists, or challenge the notion of academic autonomy. It does however, require what for some may be a change or extension of role. This change may mean no more than greater involvement of some staff in module or course design. Within an outcomes approach the academic autonomy of subject specialists and the con-trol that they may wish to exercise over the teaching and learning of their disciplines must be employed at the design stage rather than the teaching stage. In addition to contributing to 'syllabus' meetings which determine the content boundaries, academics must also involve themselves in writing learn-ing outcomes that are appropriate as descriptors of learning achievement in the context of the parameters set by the institutional decisions regarding module size, volume and level. It could be argued that this actually gives more rather than less control over the subject areas in question. Whether or not this is the case, it is certainly true that most academics who are unaccustomed to working to an outcomes approach will require some staff development support in writing outcomes as opposed to objectives for teaching syllabus purposes. This is an important issue at institutional level that must be addressed and handled with sensitivity. Above all if a sophisticated outcomes approach, that is appropriate to HE, is to work it must be owned and subscribed to by the academic and teaching community.

An outcomes approach requires a golden triangle to exist that links outcomes to learning activities and to assessment. There is little point in having explicit learning outcomes if they are not deliverable through teaching and learning activities and measurable through assessment. Again several major issues stem from this. There will, of course, be a school of thought that will believe that if outcomes *and* learning activities *and* assessment methods all have to be explicit and 'public' then the whole system will become prescriptive, too rigid and inflexible, which is the opposite of what is intended. This is probably a real danger. However, the issue here is not so much about imposing prescription but in demonstrating feasibility. By this we mean that whilst the learning outcomes themselves, once agreed, must not be subject to change (unless approved through some public quality assurance process), the learning activities and the assessment need only be *indicative* to the extent of illustrating the fact that the outcomes are deliverable and assessable. This is not to say that validation and approval documents should not aim to give strong indications or recommendations as to learning activities and assessments: it is to say that alternative approaches may be taken where they can be shown to be appropriate to the circumstances and ensure parity in terms of quality assurance. Different professional staff will expect to deliver the same module (identical learning outcomes) in different ways according to the nature of the cohort of students taking the module. The key issue about amendments made to assessments and learning activities is that all students are aware of the changes through effective communication and document control.

### Module Assessment

A speaker once opened a seminar on assessment by saying that we could get everything that we know about assessment on a postage stamp.[1] This may be an extreme view but there can be little doubt that in HE assessment has been the darkest corner of the secret garden of learning. Dark that is, for the students who have rarely been more than obliquely made aware of what it is they are expected to show in assessment activities and only slightly less dark for academics who have maintained doggedly that assessment is a matter of professional judgment and no more. The 'I know it when I see it' approach, in which academics use their professional judgment, is symptomatic of the power relationship that has developed over hundreds of years between the teachers and the taught. It was a reflection perhaps of an elitist view of HE, in which students were prepared to take on the role of power brokers in society and were therefore exposed to the methodologies of control.

CBMS has emerged as a response to the changing needs of modern global society and a developing system of mass participation in HE. The transparency of approach that CBMS requires across all aspects of curriculum design, delivery and management, perhaps puts the greatest pressure on how assessment is dealt with. The use of learning outcomes as the key descriptors of the achievement for which credit is awarded means that many traditional approaches are no longer always relevant or effective. When success, measured as a 'pass', was gauged by achieving 40 per cent in an examination that covered 40 per cent of the content of the 'course' it was perhaps necessary to some extent for professional judgment to read between the lines of student 'performance'. Perhaps this method measured potential rather than actual performance in any case. Those who have opposed the introduction of learning outcomes have claimed that they are reductionist and prescriptive. This is no more than to state the obvious, since it is the aim of the outcome statements to express the essential aspects of a module or unit of learning succinctly. Specifying learning outcomes does not, in itself, reduce or prescribe the broader learning activity or experience of the student (normally a main concern of detractors) any more than a written syllabus does. However, unlike syllabi, learning outcomes offer an explicit basis around which both students and teachers can manage learning and assessment effectively. Within outcomes-led CBMS a more holistic view of the teaching and learning process and experience is necessary. There is no place for the idea that the pure, educative experience of HE is in some way divorced from the messy business of assessment of whether learning has actually taken place. Assessment is an integral part of the learning experience. Assessment methodology must therefore reflect both the learning outcomes aimed at and the teaching and learning activities that have taken place. Innovative approaches are sometimes necessary: a range of assessment tasks must always be considered.

Coming to terms with the 'philosophy' of outcomes-led CBMS, and the broad implications this has for assessment, may be the most straightforward of the issues to be faced. There are a range of more testing practical concerns. Having decided to express the learning that earns academic credit in terms of outcomes, a raft of questions follows:

- Do all module outcomes have to be assessed?
- Do all module outcomes have to be achieved?
- If so, what happens if they are not?
- Can module outcomes be partially achieved?
- Are some module outcomes more important than others?
- Should module outcomes be weighted in terms of assessment?

The solutions to each of these questions individually are, of course, less important than the need for institutions to confront and resolve them all according to a consistent logic. It goes without saying that universities need a consistent set of answers across the institution rather than different isolated answers from faculties and subject areas. Whilst academics can remain to some extent isolated from each other, their students under CBMS roam across boundaries and compare different and sometimes contradictory answers. It would also be of great benefit to the HE sector if the logic were also consistent across the sector. As we are some way from this position, institutional discussions remain the way forward.

In our view the logic should be as follows. There is no point in including a learning outcome as part of a module specification unless it is intended to be assessed; thus all outcomes have to be assessed. Inevitably, this issue tugs at the bottom can of the supermarket pyramid and illustrates clearly that the learning outcomes approach is a major and radical development rather than a cosmetic change. If staff writing and designing modules have had sufficient training, informed by clear institutional policy on learning outcomes, then outcomes not intended to be assessed, or not able to be assessed, will not be included in the first place. This is not the recipe for narrowness or prescription that it is often alleged to be, but a straightforward recognition of the fact that outcomes describe the key aspects of the module to be learned by the student and which will be assessed. They do not describe the syllabus or content. The most effective documentation, usually a module reference sheet, will have a separate section for indicative content which will not then become confused with learning outcomes.

Theoretically, given the logic expressed above, that if outcomes are not important to the overall learning contained in a module they should not be specified as outcomes in the first place, the answer to the question 'do all outcomes have to be assessed?' can only be, 'yes'. In practice, however, this may raise problems, especially when applying the logic compared to how we have handled similar issues of coverage hitherto. What happens if a student's assessment(s) cover say four of five specified outcomes thoroughly and barely touch on the fifth if at all? Does the student fail the module? Or does the grade awarded reflect the non-achievement of one outcome as would have been the case if content coverage within a traditional approach had been the issue? There is probably no single answer here that can cover satisfactorily the range of situations likely to face an institution with a broad and varied modular curriculum. There is no reason why institutional regulations cannot specify a minimum percentage (say 80 per cent) of specified module outcomes that must be achieved in order for the module credit to be awarded if, at validation, this is seen to be appropriate. Such an institution-wide regulation could then be varied at local subject level to fit the demands of particular programmes or disciplines (although consistency across the disciplines is a goal to be aimed for). Where 'core outcomes' that *must* be achieved exist within a module this should be made clear. (This is returned to below.) This will be particularly important in areas where awards carry simultaneous professional body recognition or in which there is an actual or implied 'licence to practise' through a vocational element embedded in the outcomes. It is important that this issue is not seen or argued as a major philosophical issue on which the outcomes approach succeeds or fails.

If we decide that all outcomes have to be achieved, CBMS still allows for greater flexibility than traditional approaches where outcomes are not met. An outcomes approach allows for 'failed' modules to be handled in a different way. Traditional style resit processes can be adapted to enable the non-achieved outcome only to be retaken. This not only creates less of an additional assessment burden for staff but also enables the student to focus clearly on the particular reason for failure, rather than to repeat proof of learning against outcomes that have been satisfactorily achieved. Furthermore such an approach might enable the traditional policy of pegging a resit mark to 40 per cent to be reviewed. Again, some might claim this to be evidence of the atomization of learning and at a descriptive level this is probably so. However, it is hardly the point. What is the point is that it is an example of how the assessment process can be organized as a learning experience *that empowers the student* to build on what has already been achieved rather than to start again from zero. It enables assessors to recognize the positive achievements even within weaker assessments. Furthermore, it enables teacher-assessors to monitor the appropriateness and validity of learning outcomes. Those that are consistently unachieved or only partially achieved, are either poorly expressed, inappropriate or irrelevant.

In the context of our current use and understanding of learning outcomes the simple answer to the question, 'can module learning outcomes be partially fulfilled?' is that it depends who you ask! This is not intended to be a trite response but one that reflects the complexity of the question. Many of the difficulties surrounding this issue derive from the way in which learning outcomes have been developed and used by the National Council for Vocational Qualifications; now part of the Qualifications and Curriculum Authority (QCA), and the extent to which its approach permeates our thinking in HE. In terms of the NCVQ, the answer is clear. One is either occupationally competent to perform an occupational task or one is not. The achievement of outcomes here is therefore 'total'. It does not follow however, in the NCVQ model, that there is therefore no such thing as partial achievement of outcomes, because the student who does not achieve the competence (outcome) does not 'fail' but is deemed to be *not yet competent*. In HE, where academic credit is awarded for *learning* outcomes rather than occupational competence, it therefore follows that outcomes, or perhaps most outcomes, can be partially achieved. Learning achievement is not the same as occupational competence. If this were the case then there would not be a sustainable argument for grading of assessments and, ultimately, classification of degrees.[2] Assessment in CBMS does not require us to throw the baby out with the bath water. Issues of breadth and more especially depth, within the achievement of learning outcomes remain no less relevant. Here is where the professional judgment of academic assessors continues to be vital. That such judgment is applied against increasingly explicit criteria can only be of benefit to both students and assessors. There can be little doubt that assessment within an outcomes approach will function better if, at the *design* stage, assessment criteria are considered for each specified learning outcome and incorporated into the documentation. Well designed assessment criteria should enable assessors to address both the issue of the partial achievement of outcomes and of grading with greater confidence. Again a dialogue about the assessment of learning among teachers inevitably feeds and supports constructive dialogue about the way the curriculum is delivered. Transparency helps everyone.

There will inevitably be situations in which some learning outcomes within a module will be of greater importance than others. On a micro level this is analogous to certain modules within a programme or award being designated as core or compulsory modules. The issue here is a straightforward procedural one. Where there is a hierarchy of importance of learning outcomes the module documentation must make this clear. There are several ways to do this. Core outcomes can have their particular significance signalled by an asterisk referring to a comments box, be bolded/italicized or simply have *core outcome* or similar written after. A more effective method may be to reflect the relative importance of the outcomes in the stated assessment strategy by weighting the percentage allocation of marks to the part of the assessment that covers the most important. Of course both of these can be used together. Again consistency is the key. Whatever methods are used, it is crucial within CBMS that they are applied across the system so that students and teachers, (especially those new to teaching a particular module), know where to look for this detail.

### Notes

1   Brace, D. (1992) *Flexible Learning in Practice Seminar,* Department of Employment.
2   There are sustainable arguments although counter arguments are being developed as the difficulties of classification in a diverse and mass system of HE come to the fore (see Winter, 1993).

*Part 2*

# Development and Implementation

This part of the book considers how CBMS may be implemented and developed. In particular it explores the major curriculum and programme flexibilities that CBMS makes possible. It considers the issues that this kind of development raises and the balance that must be achieved between developing a dynamic and responsive flexible curriculum and the continuing need to maintain standards and ensure quality.

# Chapter 4

# Standards and Assessment

Standards are important. However, effective discussion of standards issues in the context of CBMS has been, 'hampered by the resentment felt by many academic staff to institution-wide implementation of a modular policy' (HEQC, 1996a, p. 13). Standards have been important to university education since it began. However the concept has taken on a new lease of life over the past few years for two reasons. Firstly, the massification of HE has set the sector new challenges. Secondly, the growth in CBMS, with the emphasis on explicitness and transparency, has challenged conventional and often neglected aspects of the quality debate. Many of the questions now being asked of CBMS are questions that should have been asked continuously in the context of traditional courses. Transparency has developed alongside student empowerment and this has focused more attention on the appropriateness of the teaching undertaken, and the objectivity of the assessment. While the academic community is perfectly capable of holding a rational debate and focusing on these issues the debate has often been hijacked, unhelpfully, by politicians eager to demonstrate that they are the guardians of standards. This is most clearly illustrated by the dilemma felt when objective measures of results (such as 'A' level results) appear to demonstrate an improvement in attainment. The politician needs to determine whether to attack this outcome as evidence of a lowering of standards (exams were harder in my day) or applaud them as evidence that their policies have improved teaching and the learning environment.

The education sector has contributed to the politician's dilemma by the past approaches adopted. In the elite system of the 1970s gaining a degree, however merited, was very much like joining a golf club, except the criteria for joining were not as explicit as those of the golf club! Undergraduates were expected to go through the same level of pain as their tutors had done and the task was to restrict entry to the club, firstly at the input (recruitment stage) and secondly at the output stage. The pain was made greater by the mystery that the club imposed on its applicants by not being particularly clear about the criteria required to pass the degree (beyond, of course, gaining 40 per cent in each of 10 or so examinations in the finals). The arcane process of classifying the award added to the mystery, especially where such classification was based upon rules which allowed discretion to the Examinations Board to alter the outcome irrespective of the mathematical result. This was the process of members of the club 'knowing an upper second when I see it'. They were probably able to articulate what they meant as long as such articulation was restricted to the confines of the Board and not written down as something to be aimed for and certainly not conveyed to the student. If that happened there would be the possibility of lots of students achieving the class they aimed for! This would be seen as a clear fall in standards and one which traditionalists would avoid by standardizing marks through norm referencing rather than maintaining criterion referencing! Norm referencing is a breach of standards, since it makes the assumption that the standard achieved by a student is dependent not upon some baseline criteria but upon how well his or her peers do in comparative terms at that particular time and place. The whole external examining system was based upon the need to pretend that standardization could be achieved across the country by having a travelling circus of elders who collectively knew what a 'first' was rather than coming clean about the outcomes that the sector required of its graduates. Evidence from the Graduate Standards Programme demonstrates that academics from different disciplines in fact, have very different views about matters of classification (HEQC, 1995a).

'Graduateness' is now well and truly on the HE agenda, and rightly so. It has the potential to bring clarity and gives emphasis to the proper use of the term 'standard'. Standard is not an illusive *relative* concept as it has been treated in the past. A standard can be, and in our view must be, an explicit statement of value, a visible symbol, and a fixed descriptor of position. Thus Roman legionnaires following the standard bearer knew the criteria (the values of the Roman Empire) for, or on, which they fought. They could see the standard and they could fight their way towards it in the chaos of battle. We unfortunately have tended not to give our students such a clear standard to aim for. We must not expect the standards of HE to be maintained by a comfortable rallying behind our shared (or not) assumptions. Rather we must agree the standard and raise it high. CBMS is challenging us to do this. In the course of its development, much criticism was thrown at CBMS which was in reality criticism of the old HE as well. As HEQC stated:

> Modularity has made standards issues more overt and the very act of 'going modular' has promoted institutional debate and challenged some traditional notions of academic standards. (HEQC, 1996a, p. 6)

However, traditionalists have been remarkably adept at avoiding the mud. This is possible because the closed and oppressive approach to assessment in some traditional systems does not encourage students to challenge assumptions on which they are based. So why has CBMS set us this challenge? The reason is the level of detail required to operationalize a module as the unit of learning, with its explicit learning outcomes, assessment criteria and indicative learning experiences, which far exceed the more implicit curriculum associated with traditional programmes. The latter are described in 'broad syllabus' terms.

Many students received little more than an outline of their programme of study[1] and, occasionally, some advance detail of the assessment pattern. Where the syllabus is less than explicit or develops as a result of unfolding at the feet of the learned professor it fails to develop an ethos or methodology of learner centredness, and therefore explicitness. The explicitness of CBMS creates this ethos and methodology whether or not the staff associated with it are advocates of the new openness. It is a natural consequence of the modular regime. It is therefore very threatening for some who now have to face the challenge, not just of their peers, but also their educational inferiors, the students. Of course it also changes that relationship with students. They become more like clients for whom a service is provided and not 'cap in hand' applicants to the club.

The sector has therefore in the 1990s woken up to the standards problem and is approaching this through a new perspective. The NVQ movement, which is also outcomes based and is pushing at the door of HE, having partially achieved its ends in schools and FE, uses the concept of standards in a very different way, referring to occupational standards or outcomes that must be achieved and passed through, along a pathway of increasing complexity. This fixed point concept of standards can also have meaning in HE as HEQC has discovered through its Graduate Standards Programme (HEQC, 1997b). It is attempting to identify and define graduate standards in the same way as the NCVQ has identified occupational standards, not in terms of attainment of some vague notion but through explicit criteria and description. It is not possible to set performance criteria against a concept that has historically been characterized as 'I know it when I see it'.

This highlights the more common debate between the 'depth' and 'breadth' notions of degree worthiness. Clearly a flexible, student-centred curriculum can facilitate a very broadly based set of disciplines in which depth is defined in the context of the level of individual modules rather than through the pursuit of a narrowly focused discipline area (which is, of course, also possible within CBMS structures). Although 'breadth' models have been in existence for many years in combined and joint Honours programmes prior to the development of CBMS, the increasing use of modular courses, based on credit accumulation principles has fuelled the debate over the exact meaning of graduateness and the pursuit of a common base-line standard. Responsiveness has brought flexibility and with it diversity, and consequently attention has been drawn towards the need to identify general attributes that define the graduate across the range of contributing disciplines. This has brought about a debate between those who identify these general attributes more narrowly as Key or Core Skills (such as those associated with the National Council for Vocational Qualifications) and those who seek less measurable qualities which nevertheless cross subject boundaries (such as analytical and critical attributes and a general openness to knowledge and its creation). Woollard (1995, p. 323) argues that a synthesis is possible and indeed desirable by eschewing post modernist and Fordist definitions of skills and moving into 'the domains of personal cognitive (but also more than merely cognitive) capabilities to which higher education should be able to attest'.

There is a catch though. Whereas the Lead Bodies for NCVQ can observe and describe the occupational outcome *in situ*, defining graduate outcomes in this way is much more problematic, since they are less easily observed and there is less agreement about the relative weighting to give to graduate attributes when identified. This is of course a great indictment of HE which has claimed to produce graduates for 800 years and, what is more, claimed comparability across disciplines and institutions. Ironically, CBMS has been criticized for fragmenting the learning experience. There is no doubt that this is a danger. However, to say that it therefore detracts from the holistic undergraduate learning experience is based on a false assumption about the holistic nature of the traditional non-modular course. The laudable concept of wholeness is really based on the vague notion of a thing being more than the sum of its parts through some kind of implicit mystical process which the non-modular degree supplies but the modular does not. Sometimes this view is reinforced by a notion of the 'gradual maturation of the learner'. This of course is open to debate and is exposed as fallacious as more and more part-time mature and often working students with a great deal of untapped educational experience and knowledge enter the HE system alongside their 'maturing' post school colleagues, (a process reinforced by the flexible modular curriculum and the growth in student numbers).

It is not easy to see how learning can take place by trying to penetrate the holistic experience from the outside as we expect the learner to do in a traditional model. It is more realistic to assume that an holistic learning experience is best constructed from learning that has been achieved through learner involvement in the explicit detail of the learning from the start. Thus it is axiomatic that in order to maintain standards in CBMS institutions (indeed any institution), the university must first have had an explicit debate and a resolution of the issues outlined above at least to its own satisfaction and essentially in a public domain open to student involvement. More problematical, in order for an effective national transfer and credit system to operate it is necessary to have a national resolution to these issues. HEQC has made a start on this. However, as we have reiterated at several points in this book, the issues are complex and battle lines rigid.

## Key Principles

However, there appear to be some principles to which all subscribe wherever they sit in the traditional versus CBMS debate. For educational standards to be maintained, students must embark on programmes of study that are *coherent* and *appropriate* in terms of degree worth. Thus a key principle to which the CBMS degree must adhere, if it is to maintain its respectable position amongst degrees generally, is coherence. This is allegedly at the centre of all conventional UK degrees. We say allegedly because it is by no means certain that coherence is, or ever has been, sacrosanct, although for those institutions which worked under the auspices of the CNAA, coherence was for many years an important point of discussion during validation. Nevertheless the myth of coherence is an important tenet, and the unusual nature of the CBMS degree ironically requires it to pay more attention to this principle than the traditional degree.

In developing CBMS and especially negotiated awards, or awards with large degrees of choice within them, it is important to establish who identifies the coherence of the programme the student eventually follows. (A further discussion of coherence in the context of negotiated degree programmes is contained in Chapter 5.) We would argue that it must always be the institution that approves the programme as coherent. In traditional programmes choice is limited or built into defined routes through the programme. The university is thus defining the coherence of the programme through the design parameters and the subsequent validation process it goes through. In modular systems based on credit accumulation, flexibility can lead to a lack of coherence or to *accusations* of a lack of coherence. Such accusations are damaging and therefore an approach to coherence must be an important part of the thinking of any institution seeking to go down the CBMS route. Even where the model adopted is not very radical, modularity can lead to the appearance of fragmentation. To achieve coherence, an institution must have very explicit criteria about what constitutes coherence in the context of a degree programme. It needs to be explicit about such matters and draw to the fore some important issues that have for a long time been taken for granted and have only recently been recognized as newly significant.

The issue of 'graduateness' or what it means to be pursuing a degree programme at degree level becomes an important element in determining whether a proposed student programme is appropriate and therefore has fitness *of* purpose as well as fitness *for* purpose. It is important to be satisfied that the content of a proposed programme is fit for the purpose for which it is intended, i.e. that it is amongst other things coherent and worthy of the title 'degree'. However, it is also crucially important to recognize that some areas of study, while perfectly respectable in themselves, may not necessarily be appropriate areas as *degrees* whatever their level of sophistication. This much neglected area of debate has recently taken on new prominence as the innovatory nature of degree programmes especially in the ex-polytechnics has challenged some traditional ideas. As CBMS liberates the student and the curriculum, and facilitates the construction of programmes to meet individuals' needs, rather than those of the institution, some unusual combinations have developed providing politicians with ammunition with which to attack the universities. In the absence of a national agreement on 'graduateness' then, universities as awarding bodies must have explicit views of their own as to what is degree worthy. This is important, not only so the awarding body can make decisions but also so that, in the context of much more flexible provision, the student can make appropriate proposals supported by academic advisers.

In CBMS, both in relation to the principle of coherence and in relation to that of appropriateness, there is a dilemma about who makes the proposal that a credit-based modular programme of study fulfils the stated criteria. Clearly in a traditional programme or one where there is very limited choice, the university does. CBMS, however, opens choice up and makes the various patterns of study potentially quite diverse. We believe that the inviolable bottom line is that, for standards purposes, the university as the awarding body must make the final decision. But who makes the *proposal* is another matter. The amount of freedom that the student is accorded in making proposals for module choice, degree programmes, award titles and APL/APEL for example is a matter of institutional debate. Very real practical considerations will come into play (such as the requirements of the timetable). However, we would argue that the more flexible the pattern of curricular provision under CBMS, the greater the autonomy that should be accorded to the student. If we treat the curriculum as a continuum running from the fixed and institutionally defined programme, in which students by definition get little or no choice, through programmes at which options and electives are available within regulatory constraints (see Chapter 2), it seems appropriate that at the other extreme, where choice is theoretically infinite, the student should be required to propose a programme that fulfils the explicit criteria for coherence and appropriateness discussed above. This of course ought to be supported by appropriate guidance and counselling.

## Examination Boards

CBMS poses major challenges for the organization of assessment. In boundaried and contained programmes something approximating to a traditional approach to overseeing assessment standards is possible. In the traditional model, the tutor marks an assignment or examination script of a student registered on a recognizable course. The work is moderated by an external assessor for that course, whose job it is to ensure the tutor is marking consistently and to a standard that is nationally agreed (a mythical standard but one to which most academics in HE have been happy to subscribe). The results are then collated through a course Examination Board on which sit the examiners, and a final degree classification is determined. Unfortunately, as we move further down the continuum towards the combined and negotiated models, the concept of *course* becomes increasingly problematic. Students will be picking up modules potentially from all over the university and not tidily within one course, department or even faculty. This means that the CBMS institution will sooner or later have to approach the assessment issue from a radically new direction. This new direction will test the institution's IT system to the limit (see Chapter 8) and will, possibly for the first time, expose the diverse practices of the different academic staff and external examiners who are part of those disciplinary cultures. The problem, put simply, is how are the results from diverse modules drawn together, ensuring comparability of standards across the marking of those modules (given that the same module may appear in different Fields, and be taught and marked by different staff) and results collated so that

Figure 4.1:   *Two tier system*

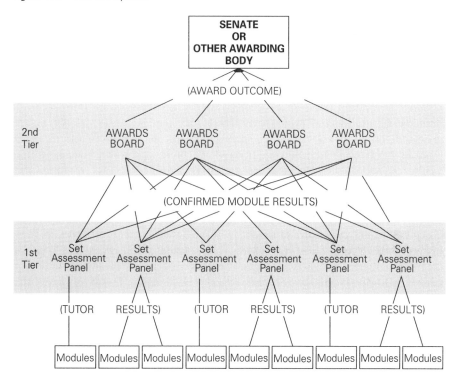

some overall judgment can be made on a student's performance? The traditional methods do not work.

It is here that we need to refer back to Chapter 2 and the distinction that we made between Fields and Sets. One way of overcoming the range of problems that arise from CBMS is to focus on the Set as the basis for module assessment and introduce a two tier assessment system. This is very common in CBMS institutions (HEQC, 1996a, p. 31). It will be recollected that all modules reside in a Set, such as the Building Set or Law Set. Thus it is possible for all results relating to those modules to be received by a board of examiners representing that Set. This means that although that particular group of examiners will not see the whole student (who might also be taking modules in business, law, philosophy from three different faculties) it is able to ensure that the results for the modules within a particular area are fair and consistent and to the right standard. The next tier in the system then looks at the student overall by receiving the marks (now ratified at a lower level) in relation to that particular student. This main Board is thus able to see the complete spread of marks for the student and determine the progression of the student or the eventual classification that the student achieves as illustrated in Figure 4.1.

This two tier system sounds fine but is not without its practical difficulties. The CBMS requires discipline from academic staff. For the system to work, the operation of the Awards Board has to be organized at university level since it is dependent upon receiving results from Set Panels from all over the university. It only requires one Set Panel to meet late, or an academic to fail to submit module results to a Set Panel, for the Awards Board to fail to operate. Whilst local systems can tolerate tardiness to some degree, and in any case are more effective in putting pressure on staff to conform, problems are unlikely to be detected by centralized systems until it is too late. Secondly, as the system grows, flexibility develops and as students' needs are met more and more the complexity grows. Each Set Panel needs to meet at roughly the same time as the others. This is also true of Award Boards which have to meet after the Panels. Thus these dates have to be centrally coordinated and agreed. The practical consequence is that external examiners and staff no longer have the ability to juggle dates in diaries. The date is fixed, like it or not. Many, especially traditional external examiners, with clear views of their status in these matters, object! As is clear, the system is dependent upon effective IT systems (see Chapter 8). The process is so complex that paper-based systems controlled by highly mobile administrators soon break down. In the same way that academics have to be relied upon to deliver the goods, administrators have to be relied upon to input data accurately; software must be capable of combining marks in several different ways and printing reports of a diverse nature. Hardware must be reliable. The chances of achieving all four consistently after each term or semester assessment are not high as we know from experience!

The nature of the Awards Board is also problematic. In theory it would be possible for all Set Panel results to track through to one Awards Board. This would then review attainment in respect of each student and thus the chances of inequity would be reduced considerably. In reality, numbers are usually so great that a number of Awards Boards have to be established. These could, of course, be random, allocating students to each according to the alphabet, but in practice other means are used. More often than not the Awards Boards reflect the Fields or groups of Fields. Where a student takes most of his or her modules from one particular Field they are allocated to that Awards Board. This is not a perfect solution since it is possible that the Board say for social sciences will be considering a student for whom a considerable proportion of his or her modules are outside the social sciences. Proponents would argue that this is not a problem since the real work has been done at Set level. We shall see below, however, that there remain many dilemmas.

Since some students will have such a diverse range of modules that no Field-based Awards Board is appropriate, many CBMS institutions establish a special inter/multi-disciplinary Awards Board. These have a major impact on academic standards simply because for the first time an Examination Board contains a representative from every single discipline across the university. It is here that many taken for granted assumptions from various academic groups about the nature of the assessment process come to the fore. Whereas in say, the Social Science Awards Board and in the Applied Natural Science Boards the unspoken assumptions about assessment practice in these particular areas go unchallenged. When two or more different groups from different disciplines attempt to work together the result may generate more heat than light. Some may, for example, see compensation for a failed module to be automatic provided that marks generally are good, whereas another may see it as dependent upon good marks in certain specific areas of study. Regulations present very specific difficulties in CBMS processes. Where traditional courses are examined through the single medium of the course Examinations Board, in a two tier system it is necessary to agree what is done to whom at what level. Compensation provides just one example of a general point. If regulations permit compensation, then the Set Panel could argue that it is the right place to consider compensation because it has evidence of the student's performance in that particular subject area. On the other hand, the Social Science Set has no idea how the student has performed in the other areas of study. We might find, if we leave the issue of compensation at Set level, that the student having failed gets compensated in every module across a diverse range of different Sets! Thus the argument goes that it must be at the Awards Board that compensation is to be considered, since at this level the whole student experience is available for scrutiny. However, at Awards Board level the Board, predominantly say social scientists (since not every discipline can be represented on every Board) does not have the expertise to determine whether a failure in a business studies module is compensatable or not. Even if regulations are spelt out in minute detail, the possibilities of confusion and re-interpretation are rife. However, whilst CBMS poses these sorts of challenges, they are public (in the sense of the wide academic community involvement), and therefore capable of debate and resolution. Many of the dilemmas that arise, including the nature of compensation, remain buried in traditional systems as diverse practice and inequalities are hidden under the guise of consistent application of uniform regulation.

### The Nature of Assessment

CBMS change the assessment regimes in all institutions that operate them. The operational management of the curriculum within a mature credit-based modular institution is significantly different from that within a traditional institution and the implications for assessment of adopting CBMS are far reaching. The first and most important matter to clarify is that the award of credit to the student is not related to the relative success of that student in a module. The student does not get *more* credit because he or she does particularly well. Assessment is related to the achievement of module outcomes and the achievement of these outcomes enables the student to pass the module. Passing the module facilitates the award of credit which can gradually be accumulated towards an award. The crucial point here is that assessment is related to particular modules. This means that unlike traditional curriculum models where assessment is not necessarily directly related to particular chunks of content in a one to one relationship, in CBMS it is. Traditionally students have undertaken programmes of study which are periodically assessed. Often this is done through end of year examinations or a series of examinations which the student hopes will enable him or her to show what has been learnt en route. Of course many traditional institutions also allow an element of continuous assessment, so that assignments undertaken as part of the learning process can contribute to the year end results. The balance between this continuous assessment and end examinations will vary between institutions, but there is no guarantee under this regime that the 'more than the sum of the parts' element will rise to the surface or be identified under these traditional circumstances any more than under CBMS. CBMS essentially requires a process of continuous assessment. As each learning package comes to an end it is assessed. There is no reason why modules should not be assessed by traditional examination methods. CBMS does not require a shift in emphasis away from these traditional forms of assessment, although it is true that many CBMS institutions give much less emphasis to the formal unseen examination. Those that have shifted towards more innovatory practices such as written assignments, mini projects, multiple-choice questionnaires, peer assessment, etc., argue that the frequency, immediacy and variation of the assessment, enables a more realistic assessment of the range of graduate skills than traditional examinations can. These are, by comparison, simply a test of memory, requiring motivation from the student only at the crisis time of the examination period. CBMS advocates would counter the assertion that continuous assessment leads to a fragmented experience for the student and that the rounded nature of a traditional undergraduate programme is undermined, by pointing out that it is possible to build-in to student programmes modules designed specifically to facilitate integration. In addition, the traditional method of the dissertation is also a very effective counter to the problem of fragmentation.

In reality many of the changes to assessment result not from CBMS but from the growth in student numbers. This means that traditionally resource intensive forms of assessment will need to give way to other methods. There is a growing recognition that traditional examinations are one dimensional and cannot be effective in assessing many of the student skills that are now identified as significant, such as problem solving, leadership, networking and work-based activity. However, it must also be admitted that modularization does place a heavy burden on staff to assess work within tight time scales (at the end of each module delivery) so that students can progress up the credit ladder. Modular systems also put much greater pressures on students. Whereas a student studying a number of different subjects in parallel can look forward to a series of examinations in those subjects within a short period of time, in the modular system assessment is immediate and continuous. The dash for the library to retrieve books that are in short supply under modular pressure and the need to submit work, probably at the same time as other students, across a range of modules, is a skill to be acquired just like examination technique.

Some students are better organized or more adapted to this kind of regime than others. Perhaps in the near future easy access to on-line library and learning resources and information will provide the solution to this. Ideally, tutors should be able to alleviate these problems by fixing the hand-in dates for module assessment (and of examinations) in advance so that pressure on students is relieved through a coordinated assessment schedule. In reality however, this is difficult to do. When students are potentially taking modules from anywhere in the university such coordination is invariably too complex. Furthermore, it is felt that although assessment details can be given at the beginning of a module to help students plan, in reality assignments cannot be started until an appropriate point in the module has been reached. This has the effect of requiring most work to be handed in close to the end of the module alongside all the work from other modules. It is a moot point what effect this has on standards. Modularity means that staff have to be much more accurate in their marking. They have to meet the standards criteria first time around and not expect to standardize marks on a norm reference basis at some future point when the Examination Board meets. The reason for this is that the mark the student gets for a module early on in a course will contribute to the overall attainment of the degree and may contribute to the eventual classification. Since the students will know the marks they achieve for their modules as they progressively build up towards their final 360 credits, they can manipulate their efforts and predict what class of degree they will get. In such circumstances it is very difficult for the Awards Board to say at a later stage that it does not like the final outcome because there are too many first-class degrees for example, and that it will therefore reduce all the marks to redress the balance. Whilst it is still possible to write regulations that enable this to happen even under CBMS, it is a hazardous and problematic action to take.

Sad to say, despite hundreds of years of practice, the HE academic community is not very sophisticated when it comes to assessment issues such as these. There is often consternation when the cumulative effect of lax marking results, for the first time in newly developed CBMS institutions, in unexpectedly high class degrees or vice versa. Marking to a system underpinned by detailed and explicit criteria may not generate the results that accord with the view that many hold about the normal distribution of degree classes. The issue is not, however, one of moderating results to fit a preconceived notion of distribution but rather of ensuring that criteria are appropriate and marking standards are agreed. This requires staff development to move staff from subject to broader curriculum awareness and cannot be expected to be achieved quickly. The alleged contradiction between, on the one hand, greater explicitness in assessment and, on the other, traditional notions of professionalism characterized by discretionary judgment, can be reconciled if, as HEQC say:

> Academics perceive that the development of an explicit statement is not a substitute for academic judgement but an important part of the process of reaching a judgement. (HEQC, 1996a, p. 19)

Thus CBMS begins to expose some problematic practices in assessment in HE, rather than creating them. This has resulted in those proponents of CBMS to be in the forefront of initiatives directed at changing approaches to assessment such as in relation to both grading and degree classification.

## Degree Classification

> One of the most significant issues relating to assessment in modular schemes, which has a direct bearing on the final standards attained by students, relates to the absence, in many institutions of an agreed marking framework to ensure broad comparability of marking practice across modules. (HEQC, 1996a, p. 55)

The effect of this absence is that students are exposed to very different marking cultures for different parts of their degree experiences in a way not previously identifiable because of the traditional and predominately single subject nature of their academic pursuits. Diversity and flexibility bring to their attention at least the possibility of unfair and unsafe practices which could have a bearing on their eventual classification. Winter (1993) suggests that in outcomes-led CBMS we are moving inexorably towards a situation in which degree classification is no longer appropriate or necessary. He sees this as a positive development that fits a mass participation HE system attempting to address the learning needs of the 21st century. Like 'A' levels however, classification is another gold standard that those working in HE and existing and potential students are unlikely to want to relinquish.

There are factors which are beginning to lead academics, at least in some institutions, to question whether classification still has a role to play in HE. The first of these is the development of vocational and work-based degree programmes. The argument goes that such courses draw heavily upon practice-based elements of study as central components of the degree; teaching practice for education, clinical practice for nursing, work placement in business studies and many other courses. If these activities are central to the degree, then they should be central to the assessment of that degree and the eventual classification. However, how are practice-based activities to be treated in a meaningful and fair manner? Whilst it is relatively easy to ascribe a mark to written work, and to work that reflects upon practice activity, it is more difficult to demonstrate the legitimacy of any mark given to the observed behaviour of the student in a practice setting. Even if formal criteria can be established, these must be fairly and consistently applied. Tutors can only, at best, sample unique events in that practice and often rely on non-university staff (teachers, ward sisters, etc.) to apply the criteria. This can lead to the accusation at least of inconsistency. In addition, placement settings vary. Some teaching practice schools present less of a challenge to the student than others. Thus those running vocational degrees are confronted with a dilemma. Practice is central to the rationale of the degree, yet it is difficult to demonstrate it can be assessed in a fair, reliable and consistent manner. Much easier to grade on an unsophisticated 'pass–fail' basis than to attempt to fine grade in order to contribute to a classification. But if the degree is classified, it cannot ignore the centrality of the practice.

The second factor which is leading to the challenge to classification comes via CBMS itself. Modules in a CBMS system are self-contained and assessment transparent. Students more often than not receive marks for their modules much earlier than the point at which classification takes place. Not only does this enable students to 'manipulate' their classification results (reach their potential or cruise along), it means they have a shrewd or almost precise idea of what their classification must be according to the rule governing the aggregation of marks. They become very aggrieved if such mathematical outcomes do not reflect the classification given on the grounds of Awards Boards' or Examiners' use of their discretion. As Badley and Marshall point out:

> In an age when litigation is an ever more present factor in all aspects of life, and rapidly increasing in HE, it is extremely risky to award a class of honours on any basis other than straight aggregation of marks, given that students will know and could challenge in court any variation from the award they seem to have earned through their marks. If this is the case, why bother to classify, rather than simply issuing a detailed transcript, or a Grade Point Average? (Badley and Marshall, 1995, p. 33)

Of course the majority of degrees within CBMS are classified. As we have said earlier, whatever the logic of CBMS it rests upon a traditional British HE ethos in which classification is the norm. Ways of classification are many and varied. Some are more mechanistic than others. Academic staff often see discretion as an important part of their role as examiners, a means of seeing fair play, giving the students what they deserve, ensuring justice. Students are less confident that in a mass HE system the individual can be guaranteed a just outcome under such a regime. Far better to make everything explicit, transparent and open to review. It is our experience that mechanistic systems which are based on the strict application of mathematical rules are favoured by students, who like to be in control of their own destinies as they progress towards the desired First or Upper Second by judicious pacing and conscientious work. It could be argued that such explicit and open processes serve to motivate students towards better achievement.

So how do CBMS institutions classify? This will vary considerably, but the main distinguishing feature relates to the amount of modular credit that is taken on board as part of the classification process. The first dilemma facing those wishing to classify is which levels count towards the classification. It could potentially be all three levels, although more often than not level 1 is seen as a basic or foundation level with the real 'Honours' work starting possibly at level 2 and definitely at level 3. The second dilemma is how many credits and at what level count towards the classification. You could, for example, have say 20 credits at level 1 (to provide motivation), 80 at level 2 (to demonstrate progression) and 100 at level 3 (to indicate the importance of the final year as a culmination of the programme). This all sounds very logical, but of course it allows for the possibility of a student achieving exceedingly well in level 2 modules and very poorly in level 3 yet, because of the high number of level 2 modules contributing, coming out with a 'respectable' degree. Thus a great deal of debate often takes place to ensure that the balance is right. Of course this also reflects a philosophy that somehow the 'final year' is more significant than the earlier years. This sounds, at face value, very convincing. However, if under CBMS one recognizes an encouragement of greater flexibility and part-time provision, it is possible that students (often mature) may be taking level 2 modules in year 4 of their study. Issues relating to the 'maturing' student become much more complex in the context of part-time, often vocational and in-service, courses. In addition, different academic disciplines have different views of the relative merits of 'exit velocity' against breadth and accumulated knowledge on the underpinning requirements of classification (Billing, 1996, p. 12).

This has led some institutions not to develop such fine level gradations and to produce say two levels, level B (for basic) and level H (for higher or Honours), (See Chapter 3). This does not in itself, however, escape the dilemma. In fact, it can make it more complex. How many of the 240 Level H (years 2 and 3 in full-time) credits should contribute to the Honours classification? If the answer is only a proportion — say 200 — then it is still possible for the earlier achievements to weigh more heavily than later ones. Some would argue that this does not matter, since the outcomes are at the same level H and achievement is achievement, whether it is year 2, year 3 or, of course, in a part-time scheme years 4 or 5. This is an argument which is consistent with a genuine credit accumulation approach to HE, but one which fits uncomfortably with the British HE culture. There is also the option, of course, of choosing *all* 240 level H modules as some kind of recognition of the 'final stage' of a programme. This 240 level H approach is advocated by some on the grounds that anything less would allow students (if they choose which modules contribute) to distort their classification by not choosing the later modules taken, thus undermining conventional views of progression. This is usually countered with two arguments. The first is that regulations can insist that if less than 240 credits is taken as the basis of classification (say 180 across the two full-time years) some are *required* for classification purposes. The dissertation modules are an obvious case in point. Equally, it would be possible to weight the latter part of the student experience by insisting that those modules taken towards the end of the programme are included in the degree classification. This is a very British compromise between the flexible credit accumulation model and the UK ethos upon which it is based. The second direction argues that CBMS is about flexibility and choice. If all 240 level H modules were to be selected for classification purposes, the students would be discouraged from 'experimenting' in their module choices. They would play safe and shy away from taking higher level modules in, say, languages or IT (in which they feel less confident) and choose modules that guarantee high attainment. This is also a reason why some challenge the concept of classification altogether. If modules were marked on a graded 'pass–fail' basis, indicating an achievement of outcomes or not, students would develop the broader range of skills that the economy actually required. Similar arguments could be made for the more common level 2 and level 3 approach. To ignore all level 2 modules in favour of level 3 returns the CBMS system almost to the traditional degree system where 'finals' count for everything, lowering attainment and motivation at level 2. Whatever the eventual balance chosen, in whatever system adopted, there remains a further dilemma. If only a proportion of credits contributes towards the classification, who chooses which credits and on what basis? If, say, the regulations state something along the lines that the classification will be based on 20 credits at level 1, 80 credits at level 2 and 100 credits at level 3, who decides which module will represent those credits? Which assessments will be ignored? In most CBMS the rules choose! It is not uncommon for the rules to say something like 'the best modules provided that the following modules are included . . .'. Thus the classification becomes very mechanistic (for the tutors) and transparent (for the students). There is no 'finger in the wind' discretionary element. It also means that the IT system can do a sweep of the student's results and calculate the outcome according to a strict formula.

Of course, the story does not stop there. In order to come to a conclusion about where a student sits in a classification band, the university must also have some method for aggregating across the marks achieved (and, of course, the computer must recognize the differential contribution that a 60 per cent mark in a 10 credit module makes compared to a 20 credit module!) But this is no different from any traditional degree classification process, where marks or grades or points have to be aggregated and a total identified which relates to a first or a third class degree. Neither is CBMS different from traditional degrees in the regulations that apply to 'borderlines', where students just miss or just get into a class. Different institutions have different approaches. At one extreme, no concessions are given to borderline candidates. In other institutions, mechanical rules operate (e.g., how many of the student's profile of marks figure in the high/low classification in the overall profile). In others, the Awards Board decides on a discretionary basis. Those that use the no concession or rules approach often find that traditional external examiners feel very frustrated and wonder why they are at the Board at all, if they merely follow mechanistic rules (Billing, 1996, p. 17). It takes time for external and internal examiners to recognize that under a CBMS system their role is to get things right before the marks are received by the Awards Board and not to use the Awards Board as a means of correcting 'anomalies'. Of course, as we said earlier, Set Panels and Awards Boards are there to standardize overall outcomes and ensure consistency between students and between awards. This is where good data from an effective IT base can be invaluable. This is very different from 'discretionary intervention' on behalf of individuals. In CBMS, students are aware of their results. They see them eventually on transcripts and see most of them from accumulated feedback prior to the end of the programme. Without a mechanistic and rule-based procedure, it is sometimes difficult to explain to two borderline candidates with the same aggregate mark why one was raised and one not. There has recently become a very fine dividing line between where academic judgments lie and where equal opportunities legislation, appeals and judicial reviews begin!

## Note

1   In recent years external bodies like HEQC have demanded that more attention be paid to the quality of information given to students. As a result the situation is much improved although the nature of much of this information remains problematic.

*Chapter 5*

# Capitalizing on Flexibility

The key design features of CBMS that we outline in this book, and the learner-centred philosophy that underpins them, offer many opportunities for flexible and innovative curriculum development. CBMS offers the potential for institutions to develop a responsive, demand-led curriculum to serve both the changing needs of the mainstream HE student body and the (often) more specialized needs of business and industry. CBMS has been a major factor in the growing confidence that the sector has in ensuring the quality of an increasingly diversi--fied non-traditional 'product range'. For some in HE even the language used here will grate, for others it is indicative of a new realism and openness. This chapter focuses on negotiated programmes and work-based learning as two major areas in which flexibility has been developed successfully.

### Negotiated Programmes

We have devoted a section to negotiated programmes because they represent the most radical aspect of CBMS development. They are not a required element in every modular credit-based university, but they do represent a leading edge of development and as such challenge many sacred cows and pose some interesting practical problems.

There are few institutions that would not claim to be student-centred, but this is almost always in relation to the pastoral support that students are provided with during their experience as a student at the university; a caring approach to students' personal lives, support for their learning in their academic life, etc. However, student-centredness is more than this. It relates also to the curriculum and the degree to which the curriculum is centred around the student rather than the teacher. This is not some vague notion that the course meets the needs of a cohort of students for whom it is designed, but the extent to which it meets the individual needs of the individual student at least as far as they perceive them. We make no claims, at least not here, for the superiority of the student-centred and -led curriculum, our point is rather that the CBMS curriculum offers opportunities for student-centredness that go beyond the traditional curriculum should we wish to harness these. The inherent flexibility of CBMS enables institutions to develop a demand (student) rather than a supply-(tutor) led approach to the curriculum without compromising quality. This does not mean that the curriculum is driven by market forces. The commitment to student-centredness in practice generates a process of incremental change in the curriculum on offer. The flexible edge of negotiated curriculum practice informs the processes of mainstream curriculum development as student-negotiated programmes lead the thinking about programme development more generally.

As we touched upon briefly in Chapter 2, where we outline the possible CBMS models, at one extreme one can envisage a curriculum in which there is no choice at all but one totally prescribed for the student as a result of the views of the curriculum developers about what the student needs, or perhaps the views of an external agency such as a professional body. At the other extreme there is the theoretical possibility of a curriculum that is based entirely on choice, with no core but a number of modules put together on a credit accumulation basis by the student. This is sometimes disparagingly referred to as a cafeteria or 'pick and mix' system, which implies the student chooses from a wide menu of modules and creates a tasty experience according to personal whim. Between these extremes are many programmes, both modular and non-modular, that allow students to make choices through options (from a prescribed list) to complement a fixed core. At the heart of this curriculum range and the criticism of the 'pick and mix' process is some notion that in order to be academically respectable and sound the students' curriculum experience must conform to certain basic tenets relating to level, amount, time and above all coherence. We have discussed these issues elsewhere, but a key concept to the acceptability of the extreme version of flexibility (the student-negotiated programme) is that of coherence. We would agree with the critics of CBMS that 'pick and mix' is not a sound and quality assured approach to the HE curriculum. We also argue, however, that we know of no cafeteria style curriculum in the UK. This is a straw man which opponents of a model which empowers students, in a real sense, bring out to undermine the much more positive aspects of this form of approach to the HE experience. Nevertheless, it is crucial for certain fundamental principles to be adhered to if the CBMS curriculum is to achieve all of which it is capable.

The concept of negotiation in education has not always been understood. For traditionalists negotiation means the transfer of power, derived from a supply-led curriculum, that is defined and controlled by the subject specialist within institutions or from powerful external sources. Traditionalists would have students buy-in to what is on offer. The assumption is that quality is assured by concentrating on a 'ring fenced' curriculum described and resourced as specialist disciplines. However, negotiation is not a handing over of power and control but a sharing of it. Properly managed negotiation is a 'no lose' situation in which students, institutions and tutors win. Our argument here is that tutors also gain from the empowerment of students. Students are able to negotiate programme content to serve the needs of personal interest and career plans. The institutions gain in that they develop a dynamic for curriculum development in which students are the active market researchers, and tutors gain by being able to use their specialisms in new ways by exploring the interface with other disciplines. It is from this that the creativity of academic life can be renewed and fostered. Negotiation thus exemplifies the creative process that we all assume university life to embrace. We would also argue that as the profile of student entry moves from the traditional 18-year-old full-time student towards the mature learner on part-time and mixed mode programmes, the negotiated approach to learning is more attuned to this development than the imposed curriculum which fails to recognize differential needs and contexts. APL/APEL (detailed in Chapter 6) which is very much part of the thinking of the mature, experienced student reinforces the need for institutions to be able to allow students to negotiate programmes of relevant learning that build upon claims for credit derived from a working context of some other relevant experience.

In Chapter 4 we reflected upon coherence as a fundamental element in the maintenance of standards in degree programmes especially within the context of APL/APEL and predominantly from the institutional perspective. Many of the issues outlined there are pertinent to the question of the negotiated curriculum. However, there are additional issues that need to be reflected upon, from the practitioner's point of view, if negotiated programmes are to maintain standards and become acceptable within the mainstream academic profile of institutions. We would argue here that to be really student-centred *coherence* itself is negotiable in addition to the *content*. Of course coherence is fundamental to both discipline (in the sense of 'subject') and the notion of awards within disciplines. It has historically been the unchallenged responsibility of the professional academic world to judge coherence within programmes and awards, although this judgment has invariably been implied rather than written; an agreement based on the shared assumptions within a closed academic community. However, in the context of negotiated awards proposed by the learner, the traditional approach to judging coherence starts to look a little threadbare. In reality the tutor and the institution are in no position to impose a preconceived model, if one exists, of coherence. We believe that the value of an approach to coherence in which the learner makes the initial proposal *which is then developed through a process of negotiation with the teacher* is a fundamental value in UK education which claims (although does not always achieve) to draw creative potential out of the student rather than imposing ideas. Learning experienced as a journey, over which one has control of the route, rather than just as a destination is likely to be more relevant and meaningful and therefore, it is surely safe to assume, more lasting. Lifetime learning was after all an approach to education that most academics and education professionals shared, however implicitly, before it became a political slogan and the subject of a Green Paper (DfEE, 1998a). In our experience of negotiated programmes, students constantly refer to the value of the process as well as the negotiated programme outcomes.

So how does an institution go about developing a negotiated programme? Firstly, it helps to have a modular credit-based cross university framework. Without this, real negotiation is inhibited by practical difficulties. For example, negotiation requires knowledge of what is possible. If a student knows the standard value and size of modules whichever department they may be delivered within, and has access to a timetable that has common assumptions about timing and module availability, much becomes possible (Billing, 1996, p. 14). Students are able to think about combining business modules with physics modules and philosophy modules. Without this, and access to a data-base which provides this information, the student spends a great deal of time and energy travelling around to ascertain whether it is possible to combine pro-grammes in the intended manner. Thus convenience becomes the major factor rather than coherence in pulling a programme together. In such circumstances the 'cafeteria model' criticism may be justified. However, the fact that no *obvi-ous* link may exist between two or three subject areas does not mean that a programme thus constructed cannot have coherence. Against the tradition of strong single subject disciplines (with no tradition of interdisciplinarity in terms of learning programmes, research or other collaborative scholarly activity) this coherence must be defined by the learner preparing the programme. Aca-demics entrenched in a single discipline are not well placed, or indeed disposed, to make such judgments. Learner defined coherence is an essential feature of negotiated programmes. Given the way in which subjects have traditionally been taught and assessed, however, it is doubtful that coherence of degrees has for the most part, ever been anything other than a learner-defined concept. It is surely a vanity of the teacher-centred model to assume that the coherence agreed or assumed at a meeting of staff is, or can ever be the same as that experienced by the students who follow that course. The transparency of CBMS and of learning outcomes brings us closer to a situation in which the expectations of course designers can be the same as the experience of the learners on any given course.

Not all institutions are willing or able to develop common frameworks across the university and they may be limited to the possibility of negotiation within single faculties rather than across them. Some who still hanker after traditional views of coherence would assert that this is no bad thing, in that faculties allegedly are held together by some degree of cognateness and there-fore negotiation within the confines of a smaller unit such as a faculty guaran-tees some degree of coherence and therefore standards. In addition, it locks the student, and therefore the funding, into the faculty which is very attractive to local resource managers with devolved budgets. This local context approach is, of course, a start and may be a move along a road that will eventually lead to a fully developed system. However, we believe it is only half-heartedly nodding in the direction of the student-centred curriculum and still owes much to traditional views of maintaining control. What we have described thus far is the negotiated award as an approach to individual student-proposed pro-gramme design. This can of course also be done on a *cohort* basis where a *group* of students can be identified with particular programme requirements that sit outside standard validated provision. These may be, for example, from a particular company which requires a specific programme for a group of employees. Cohort negotiated programmes also provide a means for a university to pilot possible new avenues of development. By creating a cohort negotiated programme, for what might appear to be a limited market in the first instance, the university can create a new package of modules which could subsequently be validated as a mainstream course in the standard way if a continuing demand emerges.

In practical terms the ways in which a programme may be constructed within a negotiated framework may vary considerably. Like CBMS itself, the extent of negotiation within any negotiated programme may be identified anywhere on a continuum. At one extreme there may be minor but significant negotiated departures from a relatively 'standard' programme while at the other the entire content may be negotiated. Similarly, programmes may or may not propose inclusion of prior and/or experiential learning (see Chapter 6). In practice students may propose negotiated awards for a variety of reasons. They may be proposed as a personalized programme from the outset and based on a clear vision of particular and specified individual learning needs that cannot be met through traditional single or combined awards. Equally, negotiated programmes may evolve as students' perceptions and understandings of their desired programme outcomes, and indeed of their personal strengths in particular discipline areas, change. A system for negotiated awards within CBMS enables students to transfer learning, internally or externally, from a programme or course that, having started, does not meet expectations for whatever reason. This learning may then be reconfigured, in whole or in part, within a new negotiated programme. The student must propose a rationale, and make a claim for the programme as a coherent body of learning that meets the standards and quality assurance requirements of the university. Negotiated programmes constructed in this way (combining say the first year of a Law degree, maybe from another university, with second and third year modules from the Law and Business Fields) may not differ greatly in design terms from programmes made possible through the more traditional combined subject routes. What is likely to be significant, however, is that the actual combinations of subjects (and/or modules within subjects) may not be part of the standard offer of the university. Conversely, a programme that is negotiated from start to finish will be unique in all aspects except its adherence to standards. Thus negotiated programmes allow for the full exploitation of the flexibility inherent in CBMS in educational terms and can also be seen to have benefits in terms of recruitment, through the provision of bespoke awards, and retention through negotiated transfer.

## Work-based Learning

There is a symbiotic relationship between learning and work. Work of any kind requires learning to be acquired and/or applied in order for it to be carried out successfully. It is not our intention to explore this relationship in detail. Rather we will consider those aspects of work-based learning that have a developmental and functional link with CBMS. However, it is useful to reflect on the ways in which the otherwise all embracing term 'work-based learning' is understood and used in higher education. Brennan and Little's research indicates that the term, acknowledged to be 'of fairly recent origin' (Brennan and Little, 1996, p. 5), despite a long tradition of vocational higher education in the UK, is used generally to refer to all activity, 'linking learning to the workplace' (Levy et al. 1989, p. 4, quoted in Brennan and Little, 1996). In a diverse HE sector not only does work-based learning include, therefore, traditional work placement and sandwich components of standard professional and vocational courses, it also covers newer forms such as work-based accreditation and tailor-made negotiated provision for individual employers and employees. It is with the latter kinds of work-based learning that this chapter is mainly concerned. It is important to note, however, that in either case work-based learning refers only to learning that has *demonstrable equivalence* to learning which takes place within standard HE sector provision. In other words the term, as it is used, carries with it unwritten assumptions about level, equivalence, assessment and, ultimately, control. In practical terms the functional link between work-based learning and higher education is the process of accreditation. Accreditation confers recognition against national (albeit ill defined) standards. In our view work-based learning will be a major feature of the development of HE well into the next century encouraged by initiatives such as the University for Industry (Hillman, 1996). The report of the National Advisory Group for Continuing Education and Lifelong Learning reinforces this view:

> Learning at the workplace will need to make a major contribution to national strategy through marked improvements in the numbers of learners at work and in the range of activity and achievements of those who learn at, for or in the workplace. (Fryer, 1997, p. 47)

Much of the development that will make this possible has taken place relatively recently, encouraged and facilitated by CBMS.

Attitudes in HE to work-based learning have changed significantly in the UK in the last two decades. Many factors have influenced this change, not least the growth of CBMS. Diminishing levels of direct government funding have led universities to look for income from other sources, particularly to business and industry and to part-time students. At the same time, a debate in education, that has involved government, industry, and trades unions, concerning the need to establish parity of esteem between the academic and vocational tracks (including learning that takes place in the workplace) has continued (Employment Department, 1990, 1992; CBI, 1989; TUC, 1989). There is greater awareness on all sides of the debate that, in order for western economies to stay economically competitive, there needs to be greater investment in education and training at all levels, both *for* and *in* the workplace. The former polytechnics, with their vocational traditions, were given full university status in 1992.

The profile of the student population in terms of age and mode of attendance has changed, as has the balance of the undergraduate curriculum, with 56 per cent of students now involved in professional and vocational programmes (Smithers and Robinson, 1995). The move towards mass participation in HE (a sevenfold increase since 1960) has led to greater numbers of 'new' graduates joining the workforce, which in turn has led companies to re-appraise the continuing education and development needs of those already in work, particularly those in established middle and senior management positions who were not graduate entrants. The economic and social changes of the last 20 years have also had a major effect. Changing patterns of employment, the end of job security, the expectation that careers may change track several times in a lifetime have all led to modern undergraduates being generally more focused on the purpose of their higher education: it is first and foremost for work (Otter, 1992, p. 33; AGR, 1993, 1995). The new scenario for fees is likely to sharpen this focus. If paying customers are expected to repay the debts incurred in becoming graduates they will, by definition, expect to get graduate level jobs and expect to be properly prepared for them. Taken together, these and other factors have led to a shift in attitude that finds higher education generally more comfortable (Brennan and Little, 1996, p. 154) and, we would argue, more realistic, about its role in both preparing graduates *for* work, and in supporting those *in* work through responding to these particular needs in flexible and innovative ways. There is greater awareness of the many practical issues concerning preparing undergraduates for work *as graduates* which must be considered *within* undergraduate study programmes (AGR, 1993, 1995; Harvey, Moon and Geall, 1997). This has led to a better understanding of the need for HE equivalent learning and accreditation *in the workplace*. It is here that CBMS has had a major impact.

At a simple level, modularity has allowed incremental change to take place by enabling the introduction of work-based and work-related components into degree programmes without seeming to require, or indeed create, major changes to the programmes themselves. It has made the processes of introducing, developing and accrediting small and/or specialized 'units of learning' both practical and manageable. However, it is the development of *credit-based* modular systems using *learning outcomes* (see Chapter 3) as the key descriptors of the achievement for which credit is awarded, that has energized the development and rapid growth of work-based learning. It is the transparency of CBMS (that enables judgments to be made about the level, volume and relevance of higher education or equivalent learning against published criteria) that has facilitated both the development of work-based learning and the transfer of standard quality assurance processes to it. The transfer of quality assurance systems and processes is crucial to the credibility, legitimacy and, ultimately, the viability of work-based learning partnerships. That work-based learning can be shown to be comparable and equivalent (particularly in key areas such as level, volume and assessment) to the standard university-based provision that it either replaces and/or complements, is of equal benefit to its status, development and promotion both within providing universities and in the work environment. Shared client/provider interest in quality in work-based learning gives both partners practical and positive incentives for involvement. For the HE provider, academic staff are more inclined to participate in developments where issues of 'standards', the quality of teaching and learning and the integrity of awards are not perceived to be compromised. For the client in the workplace, individual or corporate, there is a similar wish that the flexibility they require is not achieved at the expense of standards, quality or the value of the learning undertaken. Companies which invest in workforce development through education and training are likely to apply the increasingly prevalent quality culture of the workplace to all aspects of their customer–supplier chains.

If we exclude work-based learning that forms the sandwich or placement provision in *standard* professional and vocational HE courses, there are three further main types of work-based learning (with variations within each type) which dovetail with developments in CBMS. These are:

- In-company accreditation;
- Work-based study;
- APEL.

As work-based learning has become more widely accepted and practised it has become more sophisticated, so much so that there are a number of examples of work-based learning that incorporate aspects of each of these major types and thus the distinctions detailed below begin to blur. In addition, individual students may themselves incorporate credit that derives from several different kinds of work-based learning within a personal programme.

### In-company Accreditation

In-company accreditation involves learning that is *primarily the concern of the company or business* in which it takes place. It is normally part of the company's education and training provision, designed and provided in order to meet particular company objectives, either for the company directly or for its employees. Increasingly, companies have approached universities in order to have the HE equivalent parts of such 'in-company training' accredited. This type of work-based learning is usually referred to as in-company accreditation. Companies may approach universities to have learning that takes place in their organizations accredited for a variety of reasons and purposes. These may include the need or desire to have existing provision kitemarked; to provide and stimulate a culture of continuing professional development (CPD); to offer the possibility of HE progression routes for employees; to provide a vehicle through which to initiate, motivate and manage company-based projects and/ or research. In-company accreditation may also be proposed on the basis of cost effectiveness, as is often the case when the learning concerned meets a recurring and large scale need. The basic processes of in-company accreditation are relatively straightforward. Unsurprisingly, they mirror the key features of any standard CBMS validation or programme approval process that may be used within a university for a conventional programme or course.

*Course Development*

When a company proposes a piece of in-house learning for accreditation, to some extent the course development stage has already taken place or at least has been initiated. In some cases the work-based learning involved will be a part of existing company education and training provision. Put simply, the accreditation activity is principally concerned with aligning the work-based learning with university standards and quality assurance processes so that it can be shown to be equivalent and transferable. In practice, the processes of accreditation invariably stimulate or require some further development of the learning concerned, but the accreditation remains fundamentally a kitemarking activity. It is probably true to say that most of the early in-company accreditations were of this kitemarking type. However, increasingly universities are becoming involved at an earlier stage of the 'course' development processes within companies and are working with them to build the accreditation into their work-based learning provision from the outset. This second approach has significant benefits. Key issues of equivalence are easier to manage if they are incorporated as necessary design features of any work-based learning that is considered appropriate for accreditation at HE levels. In practice the accreditation relationship that a university may have with a company will often be a combination or hybrid of these two types.

*Learning Contracts and Agreements*

Learning contracts and agreements are a necessary and standard feature of work-based learning within CBMS. Their purpose is to formalize, through an agreement or contract, the terms of reference of the learning involved. They will normally refer specifically to the key aspects of a unit or programme of work-based learning on which the accreditation is based, particularly those which may reflect unique requirements or conditions. For example, typically a contract will include statements referring variously to assessment procedures, the level and type of HE tutor support, the level and type of workplace support, the role of workplace mentors, the type and location of learning resources available, the place and time of teaching, timelines for each stage of a programme (including assessment), predicted student numbers (maximum and minimum) and costs involved (although this may often be shown elsewhere). Each contract will reflect the particular nature of the in-company accreditation to which it refers and few would include all of the above. It is easy to see in this list those aspects that would normally form the basis of questions and conditions to be met in a traditional university-based course or programme validation. Learning contracts or agreements may be used in the context of *individual* work-based learning as well as with *in-company* accreditation itself. In some circumstances it may be appropriate for individual employees to negotiate personal learning agreements within the broader company learning contract that sets out the parameters of the accreditation partnership.

### Work-based Study

The second main type of work-based learning involves learning that is *primarily the concern of individual students who are enrolled on a programme or module with a university.* The programme or module may take place in the workplace or in the university itself or some other location, but is always based on workplace activity. This type of work-based learning is normally undertaken as part of an award of some kind and is variously referred to as work-based study, work-related study or just work-based learning. Although we have described it as *'primarily the concern of individual students'*, increasingly with this kind of work-based learning the student is sponsored by an employer. The focus of the learning may include shared employee/company objectives. This type of work-based learning is becoming increasingly diverse. Work-based study can be a work-based or work-related programme that is proposed by the student as free standing. More usually however, it is part of an award. Work-based study is normally part-time, since 'work-based' implies being in employment. There are a number of ways in which CBMS facilitates work-based study. Most obviously, the inherent flexibility of CBMS will normally allow programmes of study to include a volume of non-compulsory content (referred to variously as outfield, option or broadening modules). Where this flexibility is present with the additional availability of 'shell' modules it is increasingly common for part-time students to propose and include work-based or work-related modules in their programmes.[1] Where negotiated awards are available (see above), it becomes possible for the entire content of the award to become work-based or work-related, made up of a variable proportion of taught and self-proposed modules. The appeal of awards designed in this way is obvious to students. They can simultaneously satisfy the need or desire to gain an award, to update professionally, to refresh the theoretical or knowledge base of a functional area of work and to focus on a 'live' work-based issue or problem. All of these points, but in particular the last one, are also of interest to employers who are often the sponsors of such students. Self-designed 'shell' modules, in which the learning outcomes are based on active work-based issues, in effect bring focused action research to the work environment and, through tutor support and assessment, involve the university in the process. This is particularly the case at undergraduate level if the dissertation is also work-based.

At postgraduate level the opportunities for the potentially dynamic interaction between the student, the company and the university are more significant. The professional or career level of postgraduate students in company hierarchies is likely to be higher, their professional involvement more likely to be managerial or strategic. The clearer research perspective of masters level learning is more likely to encourage and facilitate work-based action research. Increasingly the negotiation of such programmes is likely to be tri-partite since all three parties are stakeholders in a partnership in which there are clear benefits for all. The company can see sponsorship, in the form of money, time or both, as an investment rather than a cost, in the form of tangible benefits flowing from work-based research. The student benefits from a customized or personalized programme, that is time and cost efficient because of its workplace focus, and one which also generates an award and gives potential career progression. For the university the benefits are equally clear, although they are not always widely understood or exploited. Leaving aside the obvious benefit of increased business, the university also benefits from the curriculum development dynamic that such partnerships facilitate. The flexibility often required of work-based programmes helps to bring new and innovative thinking to aspects of course design that might otherwise be taken as given. This 'updating' process, widely espoused as a benefit for *students*, is equally beneficial for the university. The content of self-designed or customized 'shell' modules may often be a more accurate reflection of the work-related learning needs of a particular aspect of a professional or vocational discipline, than the modules on the university database. This is particularly true in scientific disciplines that involve leading edge technologies where the figure quoted for the half life of knowledge seems to reduce continually. However, it is no less applicable in most practice-based and vocational areas. Of course, it is arguable whether universities in general are capable of responding to, and utilizing, this potentially rich vein of curriculum development. In our view there is no doubt that HE should be, or should aspire to be, demand-led, but the level of learner involvement in curriculum development and innovation described above would not sit comfortably in the minds of many and would be regarded as heresy by some. However, if HE is to contribute effectively to the much forecast need for the labour market of the 21st century to be both highly skilled and flexible, a proactive and leading role in this kind of tri-partite learner–provider–workplace partnership will be important.

There is no doubt that CBMS as a curriculum structure and system enables, theoretically, the development of the multi- and interdisciplinary programmes likely to be required to meet the needs of the next century. At the level of programmes negotiated for individual students or small one-off cohorts this is already happening. But these do not in themselves have a major impact on the 'mainstream' academic culture of institutions. It could be argued that in some institutions CBMS has made academic staff *less* willing to develop interdisciplinary approaches because they see in CBMS a threat to the integrity and 'purity' of their particular discipline. If institutions wish CBMS to deliver its potential as a force for radical curriculum development then there are major staff and organizational development issues to be considered at the level of strategic planning.

*APEL*

The accreditation of prior and experiential learning (APEL) can be regarded as a third main type of work-based learning since it is *primarily concerned with learning that derives from experience acquired in the workplace.* However, unlike the first two types, APEL is to do with *prior* rather than current or future learning and insofar as it is not normally learning that is formally planned as a learning activity *per se* it is qualitatively different, although no less valid. For this reason APEL has been covered in detail as a free standing topic in Chapter 6.

## Note

1 Open modules which allow students greater freedom in specifying learning outcomes and assessment and which enable students to propose suitable and relevant independent learning.

# The Accreditation of Prior and Experiential Learning — AP(E)L

CBMS, like any curriculum structure, does not necessarily have to have any involvement with the processes of AP(E)L. However, the flexible nature of the curriculum and the explicit focus on issues of credit and outcome make the move into such areas a natural progression and one which adds to the myriad of dilemmas facing curriculum planning, design and operational management.

### Definitions: APL and APEL

The accreditation of prior learning (APL) normally refers to the process through which learning, that has led to the award of a certificate, and has taken place before registration on a programme offered by the receiving institution, is formally recognized for the purpose of admission with credit. The receiving institution will need to recognize the status and legitimacy of the awarding body and look for evidence, through the formal assessment associated with the award, that the student has gained the necessary learning outcomes at an appropriate level.

The accreditation of prior *experiential* learning (APEL) is very different. Here the student does not have in his or her possession any *certificated* evidence of *assessed* learning, but claims to have achieved certain learning outcomes at the appropriate level through the experience of work or of life generally and is prepared to prove this. Thus it is learning that is the basis of credit not experience *per se*.

These definitions are not in themselves contentious and are broadly agreed across the sector (Challis, 1993; Evans, 1994). In the case of both APEL and APL, which we refer to jointly as AP(E)L, the university is prepared to recognize or give value (quantifiable credit) to the learning outcomes achieved and at an appropriate level. This allows the student to be exempted from those aspects of a degree course on the grounds that repetition has little value. The philosophy here is very different from the traditional degree programme where a student starts on day one with a programme largely defined by the university and follows it irrespective of any particular expertise which the student may already have. If there is no facility for AP(E)L the student might choose options to avoid areas of existing expertise but might well choose options which *reflect* this expertise in order to have an 'easier ride'. With AP(E)L the intention is to recognize that much learning can go on outside the degree programme, is degree worthy and can be encapsulated within the degree experience, thereby changing its nature. In many cases AP(E)L can lead to a significant shortening of the time taken to achieve an award. It has therefore become a particularly attractive route for part-time mature students with significant work experience on which to draw and for others for whom degree level up-skilling or re-skilling has become important. Essentially, the philosophy is that no one is expected to repeat learning that has already been achieved.

## Building Confidence in AP(E)L

Although the theory of the accreditation of prior learning has been around for a long time, the practice is still relatively recent. AP(E)L is more common in the ex-polytechnics than in the more established universities which have tended to be 'more cautious' (Trowler, 1996). There is however, a move towards its greater use throughout the higher education sector. Like many innovations, AP(E)L has not developed without criticism from traditionalists. However, critics have not always found it easy to articulate what in reality is often no more than a general sense of unease about students getting HE equivalent credit for experience outside of an academic, taught setting. There can be no doubt that AP(E)L is a challenge to the traditional power and control that academics have over awards. It is also a challenge to quality assurance processes in a very constructive way. Not everyone has seen this as an opportunity however! AP(E)L has been variously described as cheating, double counting and an easy option. Degrees including AP(E)L have been described as 'Mickey Mouse' awards that are not comparable to standard taught programmes. As we have come to understand the practice of AP(E)L most of these criticisms have evaporated. In some institutions the wheel has turned full circle very quickly. Many practitioners are now airing concerns about the over demanding nature of AP(E)L processes that can sometimes place a greater burden on the student than the comparable taught programme. There are those who believe that AP(E)L, precisely *because* it is prior learning, *should* be an easy option and has merely to be evidenced without additional requirements for reflective commentary or the demonstration of underpinning knowledge. In response to the traditionalists, and in order to demonstrate that degrees containing AP(E)L are as legitimate as conventional programmes, advocates have tended in some cases to overcompensate by putting in place systems that are exceptionally rigorous. This has been implicitly encouraged by outside bodies such as the Higher Education Quality Council (HEQC), which in order to carry out its audit processes, has required the compilation of paper-based data rather than the use of oral processes which, while we would argue can be effective, are often less amenable to external scrutiny. Conversely, some institutions which are not fully appreciative of the important distinction between admission with credit and advanced standing and therefore the transparency that credit-based systems require, have undertaken rather loose approaches which do not bear close scrutiny. It becomes a matter of maintaining a balance between institutional and external needs for establishing demonstrable quality assurance and the needs of students and tutors for a system that is neither bureaucratic nor unnecessarily cumbersome. If there is bureaucracy involved, this should be on the university's side in demonstrating the standards against which it measures itself. It is important that this does not transfer itself to the student side of the equation by requiring levels of evidence that exceed those which are expected of conventional students undertaking a conventional pathway through to assessment.

It is CBMS that has made the rapid uptake of AP(E)L possible. As identified in previous chapters the breaking down of large pieces of content into several smaller and discrete modules facilitates the process of mapping experience against content. However, this can only be accomplished successfully if learning outcomes have been explicitly identified in the module design. This enables the fine tuning of the map and the effective equating of experience against outcomes aimed for. The process of mapping need not, some argue, be limited to existing validated modules. They would propose that as the technique of AP(E)L requires students to demonstrate many of the skills inherent in module design, this in turn enables the student to propose for consideration, *personal* learning outcomes, that derive from cognate areas of experience for amounts of credit that are equivalent in size to standard modules. The crucial issue as far as we are concerned is that the student must identify explicitly the learning outcomes against which mapping is to take place and the university must agree that these are appropriate and at the right level. Accrediting experiential learning (APEL) is much more haphazard and demonstrably less rigorous where the curriculum is not specified in terms of learning outcomes as is often the case in conventional programmes of study. It is indeed difficult to see how credit can be awarded for the learning that derives from experience unless it is mapped against explicit outcome statements. APEL cannot, by definition, be a tutor driven process since it can only be valid if the claim for credit is made by the student against personal experience. Admissions tutors cannot legitimately operate a system for admission with credit via APEL simply by making subjective judgments against the learning someone *may* have derived from experience set against a programme of study from which they may derive similar learning. It is a much more precise science although critics may not always have understood this to be the case and indeed, in its early days, it may not have been.

The traditional concept of 'advanced standing' is based on a tutor-centred model rather than the student-centred philosophy that underpins CBMS. Under advanced standing the tutor makes a decision about prior qualification (and sometimes experience) with little explicit matching of learning outcomes and levels. (Often because in the non CBMS institution the outcomes and levels are not themselves transparent.) As we have shown elsewhere, in CBMS, module learning outcomes are sufficiently transparent for the student to be able to put a case *and prove* the outcomes have been met. This is a crucial aspect of the assessment process and one which provides a rationale for allowing experience (if the student so demonstrates) to be used as evidence of learning (rather than a substitute for it). Another mistake that some make when toying with APEL without the full force of a coherent and well structured process and philosophy, is to confuse and indeed equate, experience with learning. Experience does not necessarily lead to learning, or the right type of learning or at the right level. APEL processes must therefore be designed to award credit for experience that has been translated into learning through a process of reflection, and which has been captured in a formal way through for example an analytical commentary which can then be judged against explicit criteria. The issue for some is whether this commentary must be embedded within some written offering or can legitimately be observed through some oral process such as a *viva voce.*

## Issues of Management and Control

Many will describe the philosophy of AP(E)L as nothing new. Most degree programmes have previously recognized the concept as 'exemption through advanced standing' as stated above. Much exemption through advanced standing was undertaken on an informal and often uninformed basis by individual staff, such as admissions tutors and course leaders. As experienced as these individuals may or may not be, the fact is that they have an interest in recruiting students to courses and therefore some crucial academic standards issues may be compromised. Certainly where this occurs without reference to any other authoritative committee within the university, the lack of transparency could lead to such accusations. It also makes comparability across the university much more problematic, based as it is on individuals' decisions. We say more about quality assurance aspects in Chapter 7.

We would argue that the explicitness of the credit process and the focus on module learning outcomes provides an ideal opportunity to strengthen the academic quality processes underpinning entry. As Trowler (1996, p. 25) points out, 'where there is a lack of clarity and explicitness about procedures and expectations it is usually the candidate who suffers'. We believe that clarity will come if the principle is adopted of clear separation of power between the individuals responsible for *admitting* the student and those responsible for *agreeing the amount of credit* to be allowed. Furthermore we would argue that this principle is easily undermined where such agreement is devolved to local processes in faculties or departments. In order to ensure comparability between subject disciplines, and in order to share good practice in the context of this emerging and complex area of quality assurance, the university should maintain control of decision-making as part of its central quality assurance mechanisms. CBMS presupposes a unified university framework. Consequently devolution of decision-making regarding credit (when programmes will increasingly span disciplines) will be neither practical nor efficient. Devolved processes also make the recording of information, its retrieval and validation, a problem. Furthermore, it is more helpful to the university if it can respond to outside enquiries, especially from quality assurance agencies, with unified responses on credit decisions. For example, it would be difficult to justify a standard recognized award, say an HND, as attracting different *general* credit ratings in different parts of the organization. Similarly, variable maximum levels of APL within different awards in the same institution would be likely to create confusion and inequity particularly where programmes draw content from across a modular curriculum. In addition, as the UK moves towards an agreed credit system nationally, it will be easier to make institutional responses if there is some degree of common understanding internally. Those institutions that have devolved much of the decision-making in the area of AP(E)L are now faced with the possibility of internal contradictions within their policies and outcomes.

### Issues of the Relevance of Prior Learning

Approaches to AP(E)L lead to several dilemmas, some of which existed in the context of the traditional pre-CBMS course structures using concepts like 'exemption' and 'advanced standing'. These have been conveniently glossed over for many years. The first of the dilemmas impacts on what counts as *relevant* prior learning, be it APL or APEL. This is concerned with the way in which the prior learning relates in terms of its *content* to the degree to which it is intended to contribute.

Universities which are active in the field of AP(E)L make a distinction between general and specific credit (HEQC, 1995b; SEEC, 1996). Whereas agreement can often be forthcoming even at a national level about general credit, e.g. all Dip HEs are worth 240 credits and all Honours degrees 360 etc., what really matters (and is far more important to the student) is the *specific* credit available. In other words how much of the 240 general credits in a Dip HE (Religious Studies) programme from the University of Modcred are sufficiently relevant to the particular programme the student wishes to follow at another university, in content terms. There is rarely a one to one match between a prior award and a degree programme. This is especially true with international awards. In the UK there has been a tradition of diversity rather than nationally imposed curricula, even where professional and national curricular bodies have been involved. This makes judgments about specific credit vitally important. Some would argue that, as a consequence, the concept of general credit is meaningless since credit as far as the student is concerned is always specific. We believe however, that general credit can have a useful role to play in producing a national baseline standard in terms of credit and level. This is to prevent individual institutions pushing the relationship between prior awards and their programmes beyond the realms that are nationally acceptable, remembering of course that it is, by definition, impossible to grant more specific credit than general. The problem, however, is that there is no national agreement on the mechanism for producing general credit ratings, and therefore no consistently applied standard ratings for even the most popular UK awards. We would therefore support the development of a robust national credit framework within which general credit rating of the thousands of awards that exist within the UK would sit. We do not believe that the Dearing Report (Dearing, 1997) has moved the debate in a positive direction (see Chapter 9). However, as the SEEC project (SEEC, 1996) has perhaps demonstrated, higher education must itself be ready to embrace the credit culture fully and with conviction before it can constructively engage in a broader debate about a credit framework across all levels and stages of education.

The process of matching outcomes against the receiving degree programme is of course itself fraught with difficulties (see below). However, these are amplified considerably when the admitting programme itself is fluid (as with combined or negotiated awards) where the learning outcomes are negotiated or where the modules taken are diverse. It becomes theoretically possible to maximize the credit gained through AP(E)L by constructing an appropriate programme to dovetail onto the AP(E)L rather than measuring the AP(E)L against an extant programme.

### The Shelf-life of Prior Learning: Issues of Currency

A further issue relates to the continued *currency* of the prior learning in relation to the receiving degree. On a purely practical level another key decision that has to be made regarding prior learning (both certificated and experiential) is its currency or shelf-life. At what point, if at all, does learning that has already been acquired cease to be current and therefore able to be used as credit contributing to a new award? This raises many philosophical questions about the nature of learning and institutional and societal attitudes to it. In operational terms however, the need is for an institutional approach to currency that is both logical and applied consistently, according to agreed criteria, across the university. Several key questions need to be addressed to arrive at this point. Will the shelf-life of learning in different disciplines be different for example? The currency of learning acquired in heavily knowledge-based technical and scientific disciplines, may be shorter than that learned in disciplines such as literature or philosophy. Or is it just the knowledge, rather that the learning, that is perishable? Is there a point beyond which any prior learning should not be eligible for consideration? If so what might this be? 10 years? 20 years? Again, are there subject variations? Are there mechanisms through which 'spent' learning can be updated and its continuing currency demonstrated? The very least that is required in order for quality assurance to be consistent is for the university with each of its departments, schools or faculties to have reached decisions on these questions that are applicable across the institution.

Equally important within CBMS, where students may not have a single subject 'home', is that this information is in the public domain and readily accessible. This argues strongly for central coordination of all issues of credit and accreditation, not just of AP(E)L. A national credit framework will be of little use to the sector if there is no agreement on these matters inside institutions. It could be argued that in order to continue to be useful, a national credit framework will, over time, require consensus to be reached across the sector on these questions, and others that will inevitably emerge, as the framework becomes more sophisticated.

A related issue, which applies particularly to those areas of the curriculum that are deemed to be vocational, is the extent to which old qualifications (often those required to enter a job or profession) retain currency through usage. For example, can a HNC in electrical engineering awarded to a student 10 years ago be counted as having the same specific credit as that awarded two years ago on the grounds that the continued use of the knowledge and skills at the cutting edge of practice maintains the currency of the award? In other words there is APL (award related), APEL (student related) and APL+APEL (award currency maintained though experience). Thus it might be argued that in nursing, a coronary care award granted 10 years ago is maintained at its current levels of credit through continuous theatre practice. We believe that such approaches are legitimate if one accepts that experiential learning is legitimate. The important point, however, is not to double count the experiential learning by using it firstly to maintain the currency of the APL award credits and then to grant additional APEL credits.

### Credit Contributing to More Than One Award: Changing Mindsets

The opportunities that are opened up by awarding credit for the achievement of learning outcomes within HE programmes are many and potentially far reaching. For traditionalists this may seem like an opening of the floodgates and the potential drowning of standards. However, the opportunities are real, are no threat to standards and greatly increase our capability to respond flexibly to the changing needs of students and their employers. Within CBMS the philosophy that underpins admissions with credit, (i.e. AP(E)L), is that students should not be expected or required to repeat learning which has already been achieved, as long as the basic quality assurance criteria (such as currency and relevance to the proposed course of learning) can be met. A common example of APL is where a student uses a HND for admission with credit to a full degree programme. This use of APL is often referred to as a 'top up' route. A given volume of credit and learning is common to both the HND as the lesser award and the degree. The fact that there is common credit to both the HND and the degree award has not been seen to be a problem. However, many have not been as comfortable with the idea of students using credit from a previously completed full undergraduate award (a degree) as a contributory part of a second undergraduate award. For example where a student with a BSc (Hons) Construction wishes to use the first part of that award as a contribution towards a further degree in Surveying. Some would take the view that once the 'final' award has been made the credit has been 'spent' and cannot therefore contribute to further awards however close the content may be. To do so, they might claim, would be cheating, 'double counting', and would compromise the quality and integrity of the second award thereby reducing standards. This view is not logical or consistent with the widely accepted HND top up route, and the reasons for regarding it as in some way different are not clear. This is an example of the way in which our thinking around the major curriculum change that CBMS has brought about, often lags behind our practice of it.

There are many other examples which illustrate that we need to bring new thinking to CBMS in order to get the best from it and that we are not well served by the residual mindset and culture of the traditional system. In this instance therefore, we should not be concerned with the hypothetical situation where unscrupulous students rack up degree after degree by endlessly recycling credit, but rather with considering ways to facilitate quality assured routes that enable credit for learning already achieved to be used in a variety of ways. This becomes a more logical view if we move, as the Graduate Standards Project (HEQC, 1997b) implies, towards a broader understanding of the generic qualities of graduateness as a standards benchmark. Here, once graduateness has been achieved through an initial undergraduate award, further undergraduate awards, whether they include credit from an earlier award or not, could more readily be seen and accepted as a broadening of learning which must be 'lifelong'. It is our view that the problem some have with this is based on the fact that the market for HE qualifications is very much geared to awards. Two completed awards must be twice as good as one. However, if we start thinking of awards comprising units of credit, the notion of credit being a part of more than one award starts to be less problematic. The further the conceptual basis of CBMS is de-layered the more it makes sense. Under credit sit learning outcomes. It is perfectly logical that different awards, particularly (but not necessarily) those in related areas will have common learning outcomes. Indeed if this were not the case it is hard to see how it would be possible to make any assumptions about the common characteristics of graduateness which are increasingly recognized as the bedrock of standards. The explicit nature of learning outcome statements makes it straightforward to identify common areas of learning and also to identify clearly what is, or should be, new learning in the programmes in which existing credit is being re-used. It is a nonsense to regard previously awarded credit to be 'spent', (issues of currency, which is a different consideration, aside). Creative approaches to the re-use and re-purposing of learning that has already been achieved is consistent with the concept of lifelong learning advocated by the current government and that HE must champion in the next century (CBI, 1989; DfEE, 1998a). The traditional assumption of progression through HE learning by level, i.e. degree, masters, doctorate, etc., is based on an elitist view of education. The massification of HE and the rate of change, particularly in terms of job and career paths predicted for the 21st century are likely to make it essential that HE can offer flexible routes to broadening graduate level learning. Credit offers a practical, quality assured way of achieving this. The inherent requirement for transparency ensures that standards are not just maintained but are open to public scrutiny.

In practical terms, the context in which these claims are made is usually in the interest of broadening the base of undergraduate knowledge and learning in cognate or related areas. They are also most commonly linked to work-related professional development needs, either in terms of broadening or to enable career branching, involving changes of direction in varying amounts. When these issues first arose there was some concern, both with the concept of 'repackaging' credit and about how it should be done in practice. However, it was quickly learned that the regulations and quality assurance mechanisms to manage the processes were already in place in many institutions. Most have regulations for example, that limit the maximum amount of prior learning that can be used as credit counting towards an award. In many cases this is two-thirds of the total volume of credit required for the full award. This establishes the first benchmark since it means that at least one-third of any award must be new learning. Secondly, criteria for deriving specific credit, (that is the credit that is demonstrably relevant to a proposed new programme of learning), from the general credit rating of a completed award are usually very explicit. The transfer of credit is based on the mapping of the learning outcomes from the prior learning onto those of the proposed new award. (Where the existing learning derives from a non CBMS award it is still possible to map against an outcomes-based new award, although the process inevitably takes longer.) This enables a very accurate judgment to be made as to the volume of specific credit that can be transferred.

Taken together these two processes ensure that only *relevant* credit is transferred and all cases are subject to a *maximum volume* of transferred credit. In addition, in order to allay the kinds of concern expressed above that a second undergraduate award (that draws heavily on credit achieved in a previously completed award) was in some way less valuable, the logic requires an institution to ensure that a second award should acknowledge this, both on the transcript and on the degree certificate with appropriate additional wording such as, '*This award includes credit transferred from a previously completed award*'. In our view such public statements are necessary in order to enable credit to be used creatively and flexibly, to serve the needs of students, without compromising quality or devaluing existing awards. It is inevitable that as the HE sector in general and students and employers develop a better understanding of credit, other ways of providing undergraduate level enhancements to existing learning will emerge. It is certain that CBMS gives us the wherewithal to *stop thinking awards and start thinking credit* in situations that are appropriate and add value to the outcomes for learners.

Two further contexts must influence the decision regarding how much general credit may be used as specific credit towards a new award. Firstly, where negotiation takes place and proposals for individually or largely individually designed programmes are considered, the issue of demonstrating coherence becomes essential in order to safeguard standards. Here, if the student wishes to import the maximum prior learning, then he or she must indicate its *relevance* within the proposed award and award title and demonstrate how the award represents a coherent and degree worthy body of knowledge comparable to *any other awards* of the university. Secondly, relevance will also be conditional upon the level of the prior learning. Is the 'imported' credit at level 1, 2 or 3 (or B/H) or a combination and in what proportions? Clearly, it is essential that credit for AP(E)L is not, and is not seen to be, different from credit achieved in a conventional manner in relation to the way in which it contributes to the final award. If this is the guiding principle then decisions regarding the relevance and level of prior learning are no more or less complicated than those concerning the way in which components within standard taught provision may be used.

It is worth remembering that CBMS is intended to permit flexibility and to encourage innovation in teaching, learning and programme design. Such conditions will, quite properly, continually push against regulations and produce and exploit loopholes. We would consider this to be an indicator of healthy development rather than to signal a health warning. However, it does make it essential that universities operating CBMS have transparent and robust systems, including the appropriate committee structures overseen by their Senates, to monitor, review, quality assure and consolidate the curriculum dynamic that CBMS enables.

### How Much APEL? Integrating Prior and New Learning

In theory it would be possible to award a degree on the basis of experience alone, identifying 360 appropriate level credits against the outcomes of a current university programme. Although this represents a theoretical possibility, there are certain philosophical, political and practical arguments that suggest that this is not an appropriate way to develop. The first objection that many make is that it does not sit well in the context of a UK system that has always expected a minimum 'residency' period. However taxing the development of an APEL portfolio might be, the objection will always be that this is something for nothing. Degree shops operating out of the back streets of seaside towns might be prepared to award bogus degrees on the basis of experience but *bona fide* UK institutions must not be seen to be doing this.

We can envisage however, that with appropriate quality assurance mechanisms in place (of the kind that the back street bureaux do not have) extensive APEL*ling* is both taxing, rigorous and academically credible. The value we have ascribed to the holistic experience of becoming a graduate by a traditional three year full-time route, a process of personal maturation, has a close parallel in the new learning that is, we believe, an inevitable consequence of compiling and reflecting on a major, possibly total, claim for APEL. It is no less likely that a 100 per cent APEL degree will be less than the sum of its parts than a traditional taught degree. Given that substantial APEL claims are most often submitted by mature, working part-time students (and remembering the key point that credit is awarded for proven learning rather than just experience) it is probable that such claims might have *more* holistic added value than traditional awards. However, politically this is not a viable proposition and no university, however innovative, is likely to push this to the extreme lengths yet. The current mind set is that in order to receive an award, there must be a proportion of new learning (i.e. taught rather than the value-added new learning of APEL) included in a programme. The sector does not expect degrees to be like NVQs in which all that is required is for the requisite competencies to be demonstrated. In order to become a graduate the assumption is that prior learning must be encapsulated, gathered in the context of new learning and that the sum total is a learning experience comparable to a traditional degree. Degrees have traditionally been linear. In CBMS this does not have to be the case and assumptions about processes of maturation need therefore to be re-assessed.

There are also practical difficulties whilst we maintain in the UK the system of classification we currently have (see Chapter 4). Whilst some institutions are beginning to seek ways whereby AP(E)L credit can contribute to the classified award, the issues are so complex it is more likely that the UK will abandon the classification system altogether before the issues are resolved! In addition, despite the gradual influence of NVQ philosophies, it is unlikely that universities will want to become simple assessment centres for AP(E)L. Not only is this seen as unsatisfactory from an academic and teaching point of view, but it is not likely to be financially viable since current funding regimes are based on the supposition of something being *taught* by some means and assessed, not that something is being *learnt* by some means and then assessed. As the mass system moves closer towards a student-centred approach it might be that this is something that the sector is obliged to take more seriously.

As mentioned above, to respond to the issue of degrees by experience alone, institutions have developed regulations designed to restrict the assessment of old learning and to encourage the need for new teaching. There appear to be two distinct approaches within UK universities. Either they require a maximum of 50 per cent new learning or a maximum of 33.3 per cent. The amount of each is, of course, arbitrary and whatever the figure chosen it says nothing about that institution's approach to quality but more about the stance they take towards flexibility in course design and delivery. The figure selected immediately creates the problem of 'percentage of what?' This is a tricky issue which can be illustrated as follows. If a student has a Dip HE in Religious Studies, which is judged to be worth 240 specific credits, and decides to enrol for a further 120 credits to achieve an honours degree in Religious Studies, should the receiving institution count the Dip HE in Religious Studies, which effectively gave entry with credit two-thirds of the way through the honours degree (240 out of 360), as the maximum allowed *or*, should they *also* allow credit for any additional learning that might have taken place separately from the Dip HE either through experience or through certificated study up to 80 credits (80 out of the last 120 credits)? In other words, is the university programme of study to which admission with credit is sought the whole degree in Religious Studies, or is it the final year on which the student wishes to enrol? If the latter, the Dip HE becomes an entry qualification and the two-thirds rule applies to the last 120 credits only. This reduces the amount the student may be required to do from 120 credits to 40! Put starkly like this, the answer is often that standards can only be maintained by adhering to some *minimum* of university-based study. This is why some institutions operate a percentage rule *and* a minimum credit rule. So the rule now becomes a maximum of two-thirds credit as long as, say, at least 60 credits minimum is left for teaching. The logic for this is debatable and touches on the issue raised above of the possibility of meeting all relevant outcomes through means other than through conventional teaching. Nevertheless institutions feel uneasy about being what might appear to be too liberal. Again, within CBMS institutions transparency about the policy position and the way it is arrived at, and consistency in the way it is applied, are the keys to successful development of practice.

Another problem arises when the award aimed for changes. What happens if a student joins a university with the intention of completing a 360 credit honours degree and is given 240 specific credits towards this, and then decides to complete a degree only, worth 300 credits? This is perfectly possible in a credit accumulation system but immediately means the student has fallen foul of the protective two-thirds device having been exempted 40 credits too many, (two-thirds of 300 being 200 and not the 240 granted). Is the university to insist the student continues and cut back on the specific credit already granted in the context of the honours degree? Should it refuse any award in such circumstances? Should regulations cut out this loophole altogether? We believe that given that CBMS is as complex as it is flexible then there are unlikely to be answers to these questions that could be universally applied across the HE sector. However, given this, we believe it is vital that solutions *within institutions* must be implemented institution-wide, and not be departmental or subject specific.

Some of these problems can be overcome by effective student advice. If a student wishes to be considered for AP(E)L, is it the responsibility of the student to make the case or for the university as the awarding body to identify the credit available? This is not a matter of semantics or pedantry. It would be much cheaper and quicker if the awarding body as final arbiter of the standard of the award, both constructed the AP(E)L credit proposal and judged it. This could clearly be done with an appropriate separation of power between the judges and the institutional proposers. However, we would argue that for standards to be maintained, for them to be seen to be maintained, and for fairness and comparability to be established with those students *not* claiming credit, it is essential for the *student* to be ultimately responsible for the proposal and for the possibility of the proposal failing to achieve the full credit proposed. Credit, which exempts a student from parts of a programme that other students take, or in the case of negotiated awards theoretically might take, must be equivalent to the exempted elements. Just as students on a traditional award must prove themselves as having the graduate qualities necessary for that particular element of the course through some kind of assessment, the student seeking credit must prove their past achievements and the appropriateness of these in terms of relevance and level. It thus becomes important for them to have a full understanding of the consequences of their actions in determining the pathway they wish to follow.

## Issues with Grades, Levels and Volume

A further difficulty in the context of AP(E)L is that there has developed a confusion in the policies of some institutions which have failed to maintain the important distinction between the standard of attainment of the student (the grade) and the volume or level of credit given to the student's achievement of an award. Thus whilst we argue that an award achieved (say a Dip HE) attracts a fixed volume of general credit (240 credits) at a fixed level (say 120 at level 1 and 120 at level 2) and that this is translated into specific credit at a negotiated volume and level according to the nature of the receiving award (for example 120 at level 1 and 80 at level 2), others have either deliberately or through lack of full appreciation of the issues, undertaken a certain sleight of hand. For example we are aware of cases where students who have achieved high grades on a BTEC *National* Diploma (i.e. sub degree) programme have been *admitted with credit* to degree programmes (i.e. awarded credit at degree level 1) rather than simply admitted to the programme on the strength of the access level of the National Diploma. This immediately confuses performance within levels (grades) with progression across levels and is akin to equating a distinction at GCSE English with partial completion of a GCE 'A' level award on the basis of excellent performance in the GCSE. This would not be contemplated in the GCSE context so why should it be embraced by those giving credit for the purpose of entry with credit to awards elsewhere? The other related deviation is to give more credit in volume terms (rather than crossing levels). Thus a distinction might attract 60 credits at level 2, whereas a pass attracts only 30 credits at that level. In both cases there is a clear breach of the outcomes philosophy which underpins the credit process and the transparency of the decision-making process where students are clearly aware of what needs to be achieved to attain the award (the outcomes). A cynic might argue that this has as much to do with attracting students as with maintaining standards.

## Issues of Costing and Charging

This immediately brings us to more mundane and practical considerations. If two competing universities have different perceptions of this issue, the one which gives the most credit to a student for AP(E)L will prove to be the more attractive proposition to the market. The market does not necessarily pay too much attention to the philosophical niceties that are involved. It also raises the issue of finance. Universities are, of course, commercial enterprises and therefore the consequences of AP(E)L operations have financial implications. AP(E)L requires effort on behalf of the university and this costs money. On the other hand AP(E)L shortens the length of the programme which reduces income but also requires less input from tutors and other services. So how do we approach financing? This is an extremely contentious issue and there appears to be little agreement on best practice. There is at once a tension between the philosophical and commercial approach. Enthusiasts may not see money as of prime importance, preferring to stress the altruistic side of HE, openness of opportunity, credit where credit is due and the like. Institutional managers, who are weary of arguments about loss leaders and long term favourable impact on recruitment, want to see the books balance.

Much will also depend on changes to current funding regimes. A shift to a credit-related funding regime will have an impact on these issues in a number of possible ways. In a negative way for the institutions (but positive for the Treasury) the argument might be to encourage admission with credit because the student will be funded only for the credit achieved through new learning and not through AP(E)L. This will have the effect of minimizing these opportunities for students as institutions attempt to maximize income. Alternatively, universities might attempt to argue that if funding follows credit then it should be attached to all credit awarded by the university, irrespective of the way it has been achieved. AP(E)L credit is not free standing but exists only in the context of awards. They would argue that the process of credit rating prior learning is directly parallel to normal taught delivery leading to credit. As a compromise, it might well be that there is a middle road whereby the university receives a credit-related or *per capita* fee for the service of assessing prior learning based on the assumption that such credits are cheaper than those derived from teaching in the normal way.

Currently there are predominantly two different resource models adopted. The first says that the amount of effort invested by the university in aiding a student in demonstrating a volume of credit is independent of the actual volume claimed or achieved. Thus it takes roughly the same input to aid a 120 credit claim as a 180 credit claim. The processes and time factors are largely fixed costs. On this basis, the demand is for a one-off payment. The student might of course wonder why it costs the same to get only 60 credits compared to a colleague who achieved 150. The argument from the academic quarter is often that to be consistent with their access philosophy they should not charge for learning that has already been achieved and for which they were not responsible. All that needs to be done is to cover legitimate costs. Some go further and say that the processes should be seen as subsidizing the recruitment policy of the institution, since the flexibility of AP(E)L has provided additional recruits that otherwise would not have been in the system. This is, of course, a largely untestable proposition, although anecdotally in some areas (such as nursing and engineering), employers seem more prepared to release staff for shorter periods of study made possible by AP(E)L than for the longer periods required for a full taught programme. The second model argues from a different stance. The resource managers feel that credit deprives the institution of income since admission with credit displaces taught components of an award. Nevertheless the fixed overheads remain the same, although the teaching services are not required at the same level. On balance they would argue that the institution loses out. This can best be overcome by increasing the charge according to the volume of credit claimed (or possibly achieved). The more credit given, the more that should be charged. The related argument is that the charge is associated with the final award not the credit *per se*, and therefore the income must be attached to the award the student gains alongside contemporaries, irrespective of the type of learning experience that underpinned that award. There is no easy answer to this, since other market considerations come into play and these are themselves affected by the nature of the discipline. Thus competition from other providers affects the actual charge made irrespective of cost. Some areas, such as business, appear better able to sustain higher charges than, say, history and indeed in other areas customers judge quality by price which can lead to higher charges. This immediately raises the issue of whether there should be a single institutional charge or policy or one that is opportunistic.

### Issues for Full-time Students

In CBMS, AP(E)L admission with credit is more often associated with part-time mature students. However, there is no reason to exclude full-time students from the process. Since the majority of full-time students in the past have come straight from school they have had very little additional learning at an appropriate level for which to claim credit. This is clearly changing as more mature students join full-time or mixed mode programmes of study. However, unlike part-time students, full-time students produce significant practical dilemmas for a university.

The first is that full-time students attract some fee payment from local education authorities (LEAs). The expectation, therefore, is that students will be committed to a full programme of study. In other words LEAs want what they perceive to be value for money, which they define as students being fully in attendance and being fully occupied. Leaving aside the massive variation in full-time student experience across the disciplines and across institutions, the expectation of a full timetable can cause difficulties for institutions and LEAs who have little understanding of the issues and no mechanisms for handling students who are full-time yet not fully committed to a full-time programme (because they have been given credit against a particular part of the programme). However, students who are now more dependent on loans find the time released by the AP(E)L helpful in providing additional time for earning money to pay off these loans. Similarly, it may also be the case if fee payment tips more heavily towards the student in future that a reduced timetable is advantageous. Equally, the institutions have difficulty in knowing quite how to handle a student who may be exempted from a module in a particular term or semester. Is the undergraduate experience still legitimate in comparison with peers if it appears to be lighter? What expectations are there for the students? Should their work in the local fast food burger bar to gain money, playing more sport and drinking more coffee and beer be seen as legitimate (possibly returning the student experience to what it was before hardship forced students to combine study and work) or will it be seen as giving an unfair advantage by allowing more potential study time? This latter attitude, of course, represents the competitive HE model rather than one that seeks to maximize achievement of individuals. There are no right answers to these issues given current funding regimes. However, we would argue that the spaces created by the credit given can be used creatively to enhance the educational experience of the student. Thus students can spend more time on the taught programme and hopefully, as a consequence, achieve their full potential. Alternatively, they could include broadening experiences such as languages and other key skills, including those associated with work experience, which will enhance the 'added value' to the undergraduate programme. At a time when the whole concept of 'graduateness' (HEQC, 1997b) and generic transferable graduate skills are coming under ever closer scrutiny it may be prudent to bring fresh thinking to the ways in which the value-added dimension of the undergraduate experience might be achieved.

For full-time students admission with credit from a full stage of a programme is not a problem since funding would commence from the point of entry. However, institutions will need to establish what constitutes the minimum volume of credit that defines full-time status and to seek agreement with funding agencies on this definition. As students begin to work flexibly with CBMS and develop mixed modes of study (mixing full and part-time) this becomes even more important. Existing funding models, based on the assumption of traditional three year, linear progression through a 'course' culminating in a degree are no longer appropriate. In our view CBMS requires credit-based funding models. It is simply not logical or fair to expect students, universities, funding agencies and LEAs to pick through the bones of an outdated funding system, designed for a different set of circumstances, and come up with anything other than compromise and fudge.

Chapter 7

# Quality Matters

There are many questions relating to CBMS that have been given less than a full airing and the processes of quality assurance are among these. We intend to provide some insights into some ways in which individual solutions can be determined by universities in their particular circumstances and with their particular model of CBMS. It is interesting to note the swansong of the Council for National Academic Awards published in 1992, which, although it had a focus on credit and the Council itself was very much part of the early modular movement, is nevertheless rooted in the language of conventional courses, validation and peer review by groups (CNAA, 1992). By comparison that of the Higher Education Quality Council (HEQC) only five years later, in one of its last publications before being superseded by the Quality Assurance Agency (QAA), confronts modularity more squarely (HEQC, 1997a). However, HEQC offers little practical advice about the processes of quality assurance within CBMS, although it does in its various guidelines give much food for thought in the questions it poses to institutions travelling down the CBMS road (HEQC, 1995b). This is perhaps appropriate for an external body, keen to respect the autonomy of the institutions with whom it relates and mindful of the diversity of 'organizational systems and cultures'. However, HEQC points out:

> The flexibility of the modular curricular environment offers great potential for innovation and the creation of new learning opportunities but also poses real challenges to the design and provision of programmes which are both fit for their intended purpose and which fulfil appropriate purposes. It is the latter which is increasingly being questioned in the context of the debate on academic standards. (HEQC, 1997a, p. 30)

CBMS presents institutions with major issues in terms of quality assurance processes. These stem from the flexibility that is built into the CBMS philosophy and the consequences that result. We need to look at the quality assurance aspect of CBMS from two viewpoints. The first in terms of the systems that need to be put in place for the granting of credit through *programme* validation and subsequent monitoring, and the second for the processes that are in place to oversee the granting of credit to *individual* students who may embark on negotiated programmes or seek AP(E)L credit. The different ends of the CBMS continuum require different approaches to quality assurance, although based on the same underlying principle, namely; the clear distinction between those making proposals and those making judgments about them.

### Programme Validation

In many institutions programme or course validation processes are based around a model developed through the CNAA system and the former polytechnics (CNAA, 1992). Many of the older universities had less robust methods of course approval but the advent of the Higher Education Quality Council with its expectation for publicly accessible documentation, records and openness of peer review has meant that these older, more informal processes (which may or may not have been just as effective) have been replaced by ones closer to the CNAA methodology. Although it is unwise to generalize, basically the process looked something like this: a group of staff, sometimes within a single department, school or faculty, and sometimes from across the university, developed a course. This course was designed to fit broad university regulations regarding structure, length, assessment, intake, etc. The course had a recognizable beginning, a syllabus of some kind or another, and an end. The course was designed for a cohort of students who were identified as having something in common (the desire to study equine history) and more often than not there would be evidence that a market for such a course existed and could be sustained. The university, sometimes through processes devolved to faculties or departments and sometimes through centrally steered procedures, then went about 'approving' the course as being appropriate in terms of aims, coherence, content, standards, assessment regime and congruence with university policy and procedures. The process through which it undertook this task was usually based on peer review, in which a group of staff (usually not directly associated with the development of the course), together with some externals from other universities and/or the commercial/professional sector, who hopefully provided expertise not available to the university outside the team of course designers, assured themselves that the course was satisfactory and should go ahead. Periodically the course was 'revisited' by the panel and its approval renewed. We will not go into detail here how the external quality assurance bodies within the UK interface with this once common model of course validation.

The model works well but is suitable within the CBMS framework only in that part of the continuum where programmes are largely contained or boundaried, within single disciplines (see Chapter 2) and therefore resemble traditional courses. However, you do not need to move down the continuum very far before this model begins to break down. As soon as you move towards CBMS schemes where the possibility exists for students to select modules from outside their 'main' subject area or to choose more than one field of study, the concept of 'course' as an experience that the student shares with other like-minded students begins to collapse. One student choosing to major in building studies might decide to take options in law (possibly with law students) whilst another may decide to take business economics and a third media studies and so on. In designing our quality assurance processes we need to take due account of this not insignificant change of focus. Even if the group of modules that a major in building studies can choose is restricted to only a few other disciplines (such as law, economics, physics) it is unlikely that a validation panel can be established to determine the efficacy of the complete profile possible for every individual student on the Building Studies course. Even traditional courses have options, but they tend to be within a narrow range and what is more designed with the main subject in mind. Thus a student on the Building Studies degree might choose to select an option in the Law of Contract, but the focus would be explicitly *building* law rather than law *per se*. Those that are not well disposed towards the more flexible development of CBMS will be saying that the difficulties attendant upon finding suitable means of approving the total student experience provide a further reason for not moving in this direction. That is not the issue. If CBMS is to become an important part of UK Higher Education, institutions must find methodologies that can adapt to the new demands; not inhibit innovation.

Course designers may have restrictions placed upon them about the number of credits they need to leave 'free' outside the main area of study to allow the student some unrestricted module choice, if the particular CBMS framework adopted by the university so requires. Even where the designers have a substantial amount of freedom in this respect, there is another dimension that the CBMS introduces with quality assurance implications. Just as modules may be taken by students from outside their own sphere of study so too can course designers make use of modules from other parts of the university as part of their core provision. A 10-credit module 'Basic Social Science Research Methods' for example, could be used in courses for students taking sociology, education and nursing. In a traditional course development process the three separate course development teams would have developed three separate modules all covering slightly different ground but largely the same in terms of objectives or learning outcomes. CBMS allows economies of scale through the possibility of 'off the shelf' modules to be fitted into a course design. This is true even where the CBMS approach is the least radical; where, for example, the modular approach is based around discrete provision, in say nursing. There is no reason why modules cannot be imported from outside the Nursing School. This does not prevent an individual tutor, however, giving the module a sociology or education or nursing slant in the delivery if that is appropriate. Of course once you move down the CBMS continuum it is possible that such diverse students, taking a common module, could be sitting together in the same lecture theatre for at least part of their time so that sociologists, student teachers and nurses are mixed together.

These flexibilities present dilemmas in the context of traditional course validation processes. What are you validating? If a new 'course' is being devised in, say, Victorian Studies and a proportion of modules have already been approved in the areas of history, economics, sociology, politics, etc. then the traditional cut and thrust of debate about content becomes less meaningful. About all that can be debated is whether that particular module, as approved, is appropriate in the new context in which it is to be taught. Critics of the more flexible provisions of CBMS might argue that everything ought to be tailor made. But one of the major advantages of CBMS frameworks is that the flexibility provides resource benefits by allowing the re-configuration of modules to facilitate rapid responses to student needs. This is especially important when the students are in fact sponsored through companies with specific short term requirements. The answer must be to find a methodology that can cope with these new demands.

In boundaried and contained course structures (see Chapter 2) the closeness to traditional degree programmes is often sufficient to allow traditional methods of peer validation and review to take place. There can be, and usually is, a team developing the relatively discrete programme of equine history, that also just happens to be modular. Providing that the university has assured itself that the peer validation team is knowledgeable about, and sympathetic to, the modular and credit regulations and philosophy then the process is straightforward. It is a moot point whether traditional CNAA style validation processes are in fact particularly effective, but that is another issue. In our experience a major problem is that validation panels for these boundaried and contained credit-based modular courses are often not sympathetic to the CBMS ideal. It is also possible that the course development team are not either. Such boundaried and contained courses (especially where they exist in institutions where the rest of the provision is more flexible) are, as we have pointed out earlier, often proposed by reluctant and uncommitted modularizers and/or those that claim legitimately or otherwise that professional or other external influences reduce the possibilities for flexibility. Where this is the case and professional bodies are involved, conservative forces can sometimes coalesce and jointly seek to undermine the CBMS framework that is in place.

This also creates dilemmas, especially in devolved quality assurance systems where institutional policy has to be safeguarded at lower levels in the institution (faculty, school or department) which may not themselves be sympathetic to that policy. But it also creates dilemmas for the quality assurance administrators generally, since it poses a major ethical dilemma. Should validation (which is ostensibly about guarding standards and ensuring that the best, most up to date, well resourced and designed course is on offer) be used to ensure, in addition, conformity to a framework which is not fully embraced by all parties concerned. The answer to this question affects the decisions made about the composition of the validation panel. However an institution or individual resolves this issue we believe that CBMS frameworks will not get established within an institution unless the curriculum development procedures and outcomes of validation go hand in hand. Since both curriculum design and validation are rightly within the remit of the Senate of the university this dovetailing of objectives should not in theory be a problem. However, in reality Senates, like any committees, are capable of taking contradictory positions. Academic bodies are often more inclined to agree policies that allow a thousand blossoms to bloom rather than those which challenge conventional wisdoms and appear to constrain academic autonomy.

It is in the area of combined provision that the challenges to conventional validation processes arise. They arise because the focus of the validation becomes problematic since much that is traditionally validated is already determined outside the validation process itself. Thus, module size, credit value, volume, delivery period, award framework, regulations governing assessment, levels, combinations and choice rules, classification criteria and possibly other important issues could all to some extent or another be sewn up through the wider framework regulations within which the new programme is being developed. If we then recognize that a good proportion of the new course is made up of modules validated already, but in a different context, it could leave very little for a peer validation team to do beyond looking at any new modules not validated elsewhere already, and the appropriateness of the modules selected or developed for the award title. Not a massive task. Validation almost becomes an administrative job. Indeed HEQC (1996b, p. 72) identifies this as an issue. Modules that are validated outside the context of a course, especially through faculty or departmentally-based devolved processes, tend to be given less external peer group oversight.

It is probably worth coming clean and challenging the conventional peer validation process altogether. It may be fine in traditional courses, which start essentially with a blank sheet of paper, but even in the less radical CBMS courses much has already been written. The traditional validation model is very much an input model based on a lack of trust in the professional academics, who are designing the student experience and tutoring the student. CBMS provides us with an opportunity to put the clock back to a point where academic professionalism was respected. The traditional CNAA-style model of new course validation represented an expensive method whereby a small group of (sometimes) experts, who had spent only hours considering a hypothetical course, judged the output of their colleagues who had spent months on its design. There is little doubt that the ensuing debate could do much to enhance a course (and some egos) because discussion usually brings benefits. This model contrasted markedly with some older university models where it was accepted that if the academic running the course (who was assumed to be an expert in the subject) had designed it, it was likely to be up to scratch. We would not advocate a return to this self satisfying model of course approval, but we would claim that the days of *course* validation have now largely passed especially in those models which are based on CBMS principles. Since much that was traditionally part of course approval has already been approved in the context of the institutional framework, it seems to us that the validation process can, and ought to be, much less intrusive. Much could be achieved through carefully managed approval systems based on low key processes such as approval through 'internal correspondence'. Discussion between internal and external subject colleagues would retain the aim of validating new modules but with an emphasis not on approval but on enhancement. Until a module is taught it remains hypothetical and it serves little purpose to establish panels to meet to discuss the crossing of 't's. Clearly, it is important that each module fits the requirements of module regulations as laid down by the university's CBMS framework, but this is an administrative issue. Quality assurance in the context of the more flexible parts of CBMS does not have at its heart the validation process. Needless to say, where external and especially professional bodies are concerned the low key approach does not operate very effectively, since most of them are wedded to traditional CNAA-style processes and, as a consequence, these have to be adopted even though they fail to meet the real quality objectives of the institution. In our view quality assurance resides in the *monitoring* processes that are adopted by CBMS institutions. These are equally problematic, however.

In order to develop the congruence between the CBMS curriculum and the CBMS quality assurance mechanisms, it is necessary to return to the concepts of Field and Sets detailed in Chapter 2. It is through these mechanisms that we can approach the problems identified above. It is the Field (in our terminology) within which the major building blocks for the student are put together. It is through the Field and the way it combines with other Fields that the programme is established for the student. It is within individual Fields that students select pathways to their awards. We believe therefore that the best way to overcome the dilemmas detailed above is to accept that courses *per se* do not exist except at the level of an individual student (which is too unique to be the basis for validation and monitoring), but that it is possible to validate complete Fields and rules within these Fields to govern module combinations and to monitor their success. There will be occasions when a university identifies a completely new Field that it wishes to introduce. Let us say Police Studies. Within the Police Studies Field there will be a number of possible pathways that a student may choose in order to gain the named awards of either BSc(Hons) Police Studies (Investigative Science) or BSc(Hons) Police Studies (Community). These pathways will to some extent draw on some of the same modules in the Field. There will also be the possibility of students taking some specific modules in the Field and combining them with those of another Field to gain a combined award of Police Studies *with* or *and* e.g. Philosophy. What is the validation job here? This depends. It might well be that all, or the vast majority, of the modules in this new Field are themselves new. In this case it is probably worthwhile gathering together the traditional CNAA style group to approve the new Field by agreeing the modules and most importantly the combination of modules (or Field rules) which contribute to the named pathways. However, it is possible that many of the modules are already in existence from other Fields within the university (criminology, social policy, applied sciences, etc.) In this case the job is less complex and requires a procedure whereby the university can assure itself that these existing modules are suitable for the new Field and the proposed combination of modules (Field rules) is satisfactory. This does not require the old style CNAA panel and indeed could be accomplished by correspondence with one or two external experts if sufficient trust were placed upon the staff developing the programme. It is, after all, still just a hypothetical programme until it has been delivered. This process can be undertaken within the overall purview of an academic standards committee reporting to Senate and ensuring that appropriate criteria are being applied and being met.

The great advantage of CBMS is its flexibility and speed of responsiveness. It might well be that the university has no need to develop a new Field at all, but merely needs to add to an existing Field some new modules to produce a new combination of modules for a new pathway. Here again it is a matter of finding a mechanism to approve the modules and the combination. The modules may not be new at all but pre-existing in a different context which makes the job even less problematic. The question simply becomes, 'is this already approved module, when combined with these modules, appropriate to lead to the award of Police Studies (Forensics)?' This hardly requires a full validation process. It does, however, bring to light an interesting curriculum issue. Subject staff find it very taxing to find ways of describing their modules in ways that are not context specific. Thus in developing the module 'Introduction to Contract Law', lawyers will write the learning outcomes in such a way that the Building department and the Business Studies department have the urge to develop their own 'Introductions'. In addition, there are still many unresolved intellectual property issues relating to module design, in that staff sometimes feel aggrieved if *their* module is used by other people. Module ownership is something that CBMS institutions will need to resolve. However, in theory, and more and more in practice, module sharing can bring about huge savings in development time and consequently in validation activity.

In summary then, CBMS requires a radical overhaul of the validation approaches that built up in the context of traditional courses especially under the tutorship of the CNAA. Ironically, the older universities are attempting to meet the allegedly more rigorous approaches of new external bodies like the new QAA by adopting some of those procedures. What is needed is a return to the approaches adopted by those universities in the past. Here professional standards were applied to course (module) content and administrators, through the office of the Registrar, ensured conformity to university regulations. Something very similar is then required in the new context of the more flexible CBMS programmes, albeit under the watchful eye of a Senate's academic standards machinery. There must remain a concern, however, that external bodies with a remit for quality assurance nationally continue to see CBMS as a minority interest and establish their own procedures on assumptions which generally no longer hold true.

### Individual Student Validation

Much of what has been described above results from the flexibility of CBMS. Such flexibility is taken to an extreme in the case of students who register on negotiated awards. The quality assurance issues are nevertheless just as significant and the solutions, especially in respect of the validation of their programmes need careful attention. As HEQC says:

> Credit-based systems of learning may require a certain revision of thinking about the overall approach to aspects of quality assurance. In terms of approval, the general issues will, in many areas be identical to that for a traditional 'programmatic' (i.e. fixed menu) course. (HEQC, 1995b, p. 7)

In other parts of the CBMS continuum, as we detailed above, the focus of validation is on the university, its Fields (Field rules), pathways, modules, regulations, etc. Here the end product is university owned which for the sake of argument we shall call a course leading to a named award. In the case of the negotiated programme, there is essentially a blank sheet of paper for each individual student embarking on the experience. Nevertheless, what is written eventually on the paper by the student must adhere to the academic norms relating to degrees in the UK in terms of standards, level, coherence and the like. In addition, the student will be aiming for a BA or BSc with some kind of title that describes the learning experience. The university must have processes for validating the student's proposals against both these aspects in accordance with university regulations. Whilst there is a need for a loosening of traditional validation processes generally, in relation to negotiated awards a fairly prescriptive model with appropriate safeguards built into the university's systems is required. The logic is consistent. We argued for a greater recognition of the professionalism of academic staff in creating modules overseen by objective and separate internal quality assurance bodies. We argue here the appropriateness of putting the onus on students to prove their case, against explicit criteria, in the context of negotiated awards. This requires a three cornered relationship in negotiated award and related AP(E)L approval: the student, the student's academic adviser, and the university. In the same way that most institutions have academic standards committees, which oversee course validation processes, we believe it is essential for them to have parallel committees with similar responsibilities for the approval of individually negotiated programmes of study including AP(E)L. We would expect that a student with *guidance* from an academic counsellor would be required to propose the title of the award that is being sought (one which was not available through normal course provision), the combination of modules that would be needed to achieve the necessary outcomes for that title (subject to the constraints of availability, timetables and sequencing rules) and make a case for that unique award in terms of conventional academic requirements relating to aims, coherence and standards. Such a proposal alongside any claims for APL/APEL would need to be considered by an objective and separate committee divorced from the guidance process.

A crucial issue for an institution is whether such a committee should be part of the central processes of the university or devolved to faculty or departmental level. It is possible to have a cross university framework but to control and manage it in a devolved manner through local processes. In other words, negotiation can go on locally and approval mechanisms for programmes can be undertaken locally (possibly using institutionally agreed criteria). Alternatively, the process of negotiation and approval can be managed centrally with local departments providing support. Both models operate in the UK and have their advantages and disadvantages. The advantage of the devolved model is that tutors at the local level feel that that they retain ownership of the process and it fits into the 1990s ideology of devolution and empowerment. It is possible to operate such a devolved system, some would argue effectively, in quality terms, by establishing appropriate quality committees involving peers from the wider institution. However, in our view the disadvantages by far outweigh the advantages. The localized system functions to minimize true choice for the student by limiting the perception of both staff and students predominantly to the offerings at local level. In quality terms, there remains the large possibility that several locally-based quality committees are taking different decisions about the same issues and developing an inconsistent policy for the institution. This becomes problematic when internal and external audit processes are undertaken. It also causes confusion for potential students who do not know exactly at what point in the organization to make contact.

A centralized model is more effective, efficient and true to the philosophy of CBMS processes provided that local tutors play a central role. Collaboration between centre and local tutors is essential and indeed no centrally overseen model can operate without this. As a principle, this is as important as student empowerment. The need is to gain the confidence of local tutors so that they understand that the 'centre' is not taking over the world but seeking to maximize student opportunities through the local faculty or department. In our experience, once this is fully understood local departments embrace negotiated programmes, identifying them as a means of increasing rather than diminishing student numbers. Central control and management empower the student and, since negotiated programmes are student-centred by definition, this argues strongly for a single point of contact through which to initiate and manage the process. Through student empowerment the student is a crucial element in this collaborative process between department and centre, a process which itself adds value to the student's HE experience. Thus there are various approaches to maintaining standards in negotiated programmes, according to the degree to which institutional policy has developed. Some departmentally-based approaches make use either of a special sub-committee of their local academic standards committee or of the departmental board. Others make use of the pre-existing Examinations or Awards Board. By giving the Examinations Board a dual function in this way, and because it already has external examiners from other institutions present, it is argued that this committee is in a good position to decide whether a proposal for a negotiated programme, including APL/APEL, meets the required standards of the university. However, if the negotiated award programme is a cross university system, such local processes act as an inhibitor to true flexibility. For the reason identified above, some institutions opt for a more centralized system. The key issue for the university then becomes whether this committee should be,

- the university's current Academic Standards Committee (or equivalent);
- a specialist sub-committee of the Academic Standards Committee; or
- a specialist sub-committee reporting direct to Senate itself.

Much depends on the amount of work generated and the number of students. Once flexible, negotiated provision has been established it tends to generate a market beyond the expectations of those who are responsible for it. Not only are students attracted to it, but staff, initially reluctant, start seeing the benefits. They recognize the income generating potential of negotiated cohort programmes for local business and industry. In addition, they also see the negotiated award as a means of solving other problems. Well motivated and otherwise sound students who are failing to achieve their potential because of poor choices in their original standard degree programme can be transferred (subject to regulatory controls) and not be lost to the university. This satisfies student-centred tutors, who are reluctant to see the early demise of a promising student who has used up all conventional means of survival. As numbers rise, it soon becomes apparent that the university's central Academic Standards Committee, that *inter alia* approves conventional awards through the standard validation and review processes, does not have the capacity to handle the influx of negotiated awards.

For this reason it is the case that some institutions form a purpose designed university committee which we will call here the University Credit Approvals Board (UCAB). This then takes on the responsibility for approving negotiated programmes, APL and APEL, university-wide. The issue then becomes whether this committee should report directly to Senate or remain a sub-committee of the university's Academic Standards Committee. On the one hand, reporting direct to Senate gives the whole area of curriculum flexibility, and the possibilities it generates, a much higher profile within the institution. This might be considered appropriate especially in the early days of development within the institution. On the other hand, it is also vitally important to confirm, internally and externally, that the negotiated degree is no different in terms of standards and quality compared from the conventional degree. There should be no special provisions which might lead to accusations that these degrees are inferior. For this reason making UCAB a sub-committee of the university's Academic Standards Committee gives out an equally valuable set of signals. There may, however, be one area where some variation of practice may occur in respect of the approval of negotiated awards. It is not uniform practice in the UK for university Academic Standards Committees to have representatives from other universities on them. Given the nature of negotiated awards and the fact that currently they sit in a 'political' arena, it is often helpful to have at least one and maybe more academics from other institutions present as full members. UCAB will receive from each applicant a programme proposal, a proposed award title, and recommendations from at least one independent evaluator. Such independent evaluators need not be external to the university, (although they may well have to be on certain occasions given the nature of the proposal). They must, however, be independent in the sense that they do not benefit from a successful outcome in the way an admissions tutor or resource manager might, by increasing the recruitment to their modules! The role of UCAB is to ensure that there is consistency of treatment, application of regulations, and a secure rationale for the proposal. Given the composition of UCAB, comprising academics from across the university as well as externals, debates will be lively. Departmentally-based conventional wisdoms may become highly contentious but will also contribute to the debate.

## Monitoring

If course validation is problematic, so too is course monitoring. In the same way that it is difficult to identify the nature of the beast to be validated, it is equally problematic to identify the basis by which the ongoing quality of the provision will be monitored. Traditionally this has been done through course committees, which have evaluated the student experience through student questionnaires and other forms of student feedback, identified trends in student assessment outcomes, focused on external examiner reports, etc. Since the concept of course is much more fragile in CBMS, then the target for evaluation and the point and place of evaluation is rendered problematic. If there are almost as many courses as there are students then monitoring becomes a resource intensive affair and probably not cost effective. Again there are no right answers to this problem. But we need to approach the issue from a different perspective. If the concept of courses is no longer meaningful we should not attempt to monitor something that looks like a course. Here we need to reintroduce the concept of Set. In Chapter 2 we stated that an institution needed to place modules in one place organizationally in order to facilitate its resourcing and quality management; the Module Set (a place where all cognate modules are located). Thus there may be a Set for example for law. This provides us with an opportunity to evaluate the delivery of law modules across the institution no matter in which Fields the module may be located. Thus student evaluation at module level can be fed into the university monitoring system via the Set.

The students' views on the delivery of that module in different Fields by different staff can be compared and contrasted, the comparative resourcing of the module can be assessed. Since Sets also relate to assessment processes (see Chapter 4) then student achievement can be evaluated and the necessary cross referencing undertaken. External examiners' observations can be fed into the system. Thus not only can a picture of the adequacy of a module be built up over time, either in relation to a particular Field delivery or as a university module *per se*, but the whole of a Set can be evaluated so the university can

Figure 7.1: Illustration of the module set

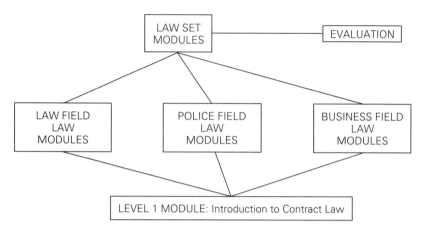

ascertain the quality of the delivery of, say, law as a subject right across the institution. But quality is not just about overseeing standards. It should be about enhancing those standards. Sets are not only the basis for collecting together cognate modules, they could also be the basis for subject-based development of staff from different parts of the university giving them a focus for joining together in a network which crosses the rigid boundaries of department and faculty. The previously isolated lawyer in the Building department gets an opportunity to interact with colleagues other than builders. Monitoring at Set level also provides the basis for monitoring at Field and student pathway level. One can get a feel for the quality of provision for any particular group of students taking modules within that Field by re-combining the views of staff, students and others on the quality of module delivery obtained for Set purposes. If required this can be done even down to the pathway level of an individual student.

This is not the same as traditional course evaluation. We must accept that CBMS delivers a different kind of curriculum and therefore allows a different kind of monitoring and evaluation. Diversity in student choice means that discrete courses no longer exist and that some bulking up of monitoring through Fields will have to suffice. This is not to say that monitoring cannot be done at an individual student level, but the further along the continuum towards very flexible programmes the more problematic this becomes and the more costly. However, this does not mean that the method of monitoring should not fit into the normal processes of institutional annual monitoring. Evaluation based on Sets is capable of being overseen at an institutional level. CBMS does not mean that the university loses any feel for the quality of its provision. Thus reports at Set level, as well as being received by schools, faculties or departments for action should be received by university-wide committees such as the academic standards committees of Senates. This will enable the institution to identify issues which relate to several different Sets as well as those within a particular Set. Thus it may well be that the evaluation of the Law Set suggests that students are being over assessed (incidentally a very common problem with modular programmes). It may just be the case that this same issue arises in respect of the History Set and Business Set, suggesting that there is a wider issue for debate and resolution. Detecting such wider issues will only be successful if the university, through its cross institutional committees, provides some guidance about what issues might be reflected upon at module and Set level. In the collation of statistics on assessment, for example, common issues can be identified. Since this is centrally managed, performance indicators can be fairly easily established. In receiving comments from external examiners, however, this will only happen if the latter are encouraged or required to focus on certain key issues in the reports they are asked to produce. HEQC has identified that in many institutions guidelines or proformas have been introduced with a view to establishing this good practice. These have themselves been under scrutiny, however, since, some argue, they can limit the external's input as well as encourage it (HEQC, 1996c, p. 26). CBMS encourages a consistency in approach but at the same time institutions must prevent such consistency becoming slavish conformity.

It is in the area of student feedback at module and Set level for the purposes of monitoring that the issues are most complex. Many institutions have moved towards producing guidelines for the production of student questionnaires and the analysis of the results (HEQC, 1996b, p. 52) in order to achieve some consistency of approach and common issues for feedback. The problem resides, however, in the sheer weight of information that it is possible to derive from students. If every module was monitored at the end of each delivery period of a term or semester on the basis of each student completing a questionnaire, the amount of time and energy, let alone paper and computer power, engaged in this activity would far outweigh any benefit that might be derived! For this reason other strategies are sometimes deployed. These are no different from those that might be used in traditional courses, but their use presents special problems given the fragmented nature of the 'course'. Such devices include the use of module group, or cohort, responses rather than individual student views. This has the advantage of reducing the number of responses but requires individual views to be mediated via a tutor, or a student representative, who fills in a form or paraphrases views. Either way it presents a low level filter mechanism and the beginnings of a series of 'rounding-up' of comments which can lead to blandness. Another way is for the institution to be selective about its monitoring. Rather than doing all Sets and therefore all modules every term, semester or year, the university establishes a rolling programme and over a period of time works its way through its Sets. This could be on a cognate Set basis (taking all the Sets and therefore modules that are associated with say science and technology areas) or it could be that a decision is made to select Sets deliberately because they spread across the university's offering. Whichever the approach, the criticism is often made that since students under more flexible CBMS regimes do not belong, except at module level, to anything resembling a united group of students there is no real integrated approach to their experience. This may at the end of the day be true. If 4000 students are essentially taking 4000 different courses it is unlikely that a form of evaluation can be devised that is sufficiently student-focused to meet the old criteria. Traditional forms of evaluation focused on *courses* because courses and student groups were in close alignment. We can attempt to ameliorate some of these problems. Some institutions use university-wide questionnaires based on stratified random samples to get to grips with issues. These are less module focused but reflect upon the total student experience. This is not ideal since it has the disadvantage that all such sampling approaches have. Nevertheless, as part of the evaluation armoury it has a role to play. Another approach is through the establishment of university-wide student panels at, say, undergraduate and postgraduate levels which can act as liaison groups to convey the nuances of the student concerns and to debate the outcomes of the somewhat blunter instrument of the questionnaire.

However a university approaches and resolves these dilemmas it is clear it will not have a free hand. Quality and standards are high on the political agenda in the UK and much activity will be undertaken in order to show, not that quality processes are effective, but that they are seen to be by external bodies. Unfortunately, the most effective methods for maintaining standards are not always those that are susceptible to such evidencing.

# Chapter 8

# Managing and Resourcing CBMS

### Information Technology

Like it or not, information technology is a central part of the operation of any course within a university whether it is a traditional non-modular and non-credit-based institution or at some point along the CBMS continuum. The sheer weight of student numbers usually necessitates some form of IT operation and of course the requirements of the university or outside bodies usually reinforce that need. CBMS is no different. However, the further along the CBMS continuum one moves the more complex the nature of the teaching and learning framework and the more important the need for IT, as previous chapters have shown. There are a number of key applications for IT, some or all of which are used by universities to operate their CBMS frameworks. There are some key *input* factors which are common to all institutions. For example, the identification of a student on a particular award. There are key *output* factors used by all institutions, such as linking that student with a particular award (e.g. BSc(Hons) Biology). However, CBMS institutions more often than not have to take the IT processes several stages further if they are to provide the flexibility they set out to offer students and staff.

### *Registration*

All universities use IT for the purposes of registering their students and enrolling them on courses. However, since we have shown the concept of course is much more fragile, by definition, the tracking of the student has to operate at module level. Given the number of students in any one institution and the number of modules which can potentially combine, IT is the only realistic way of facilitating genuine flexibility. Without this students would need to be restricted to a narrower range of choices. Thus student identification is important for any system. The IT system for the CBMS institution must link that identification not only with the registration of the student on a particular module and group of modules but must also supply to the student the description of the module so that choice can be made. Whereas in less flexible models the student might be aware that they are studying biology of a certain type and that this is described in the prospectus, in the CBMS institution the descriptors at the level of the module take on a major significance. It is impractical and inefficient to retain a paper-based system.

*Timetabling*

The IT system plays a special role in the timetable. Whereas in a conventional institution the timetable can often be established through historical precedent and is invariably contained within a department or faculty, the CBMS institution has to go beyond the level of the course and develop processes for constructing a student timetable, often unique to that individual. Of course this is a matter of degree. Most institutions aim to promote a non-clashing timetable to accommodate programmes like combined honours, but in CBMS the approach is not from the course perspective but from the student's perspective. Timetabling in CBMS needs to bring all information into the public domain at institutional level. For example some CBMS institutions seek to maximize opportunities for mature students with children by attempting to timetable their provision within a shorter day, rather than timetabling a course and then offering it to the student as a possible choice. This can only be done where there is central control over such factors as timetable slots, and where there is a real awareness of the potential of CBMS at an institutional level. This can only be achieved through effective IT systems.

*Assessment and Conferment*

Of course the more flexible the students' timetables the more complex the assessment and conferments processes. As we have shown previously, the movement of student grades around the system (so that they can be awarded the appropriate degree through a Set Panel and Awards Board) is itself a highly complex affair which must be coordinated so that everything happens on time. In a traditional system, where assessment often operates within tighter boundaries (of a pre-defined nature), paper-based approaches are still viable and IT is often used only for the recording of grades for the registry. In CBMS, information technology is part of the process of not only recording data but moving that data around a complex and overlapping system as outlined in Chapter 4. In addition, since transcripts are an integral part of CBMS, providing at the very least a statement of modules studied and at best meeting the requirements of Dearing's Progress File (Dearing, 1997, p. 141), IT is an essential element in capturing the information which will accompany the student's Award Certificate.

So what issues arise for the institution determined to go down the CBMS road? The first dilemma facing the CBMS institution is the expectation that staff have of the IT system, which manages the framework with which they are so intimately related in their everyday academic lives. Staff often have schizophrenic approaches and may use these to political effect within the institution. On the one hand they have an overt and declared view that the IT system will run the framework to good effect. This is also the view of institutional managers in introducing both the IT system and the model of CBMS. On the other hand, both staff and managers know full well that on an everyday basis the IT may not deliver! This is not just a matter for CBMS but is symptomatic of the unrealistic expectation that IT will deliver against a backdrop of a number of underlying problems:

- inadequate and/or inappropriate investment;
- control vested in the hands of technocrats;
- inexperienced academics and administrators;
- software suppliers who reinforce unrealistic expectations.

Although IT is at the heart of a successful CBMS institution, it is neither the software nor the hardware that is crucial. It is the people who design and operate the IT systems that are crucial to success, i.e. academics, technocrats, administrators, students and managers.

We have stated elsewhere that the more flexible the curriculum the more rigid the management and control frameworks that surround the curriculum. There is an direct relationship between flexibility and control. The less flexible the curriculum, the less need for centralized managerial and administrative control over such matters as the timetable, marking schemes, and so forth. The IT system plays a vital part in any firm system of management and control. Computers do not allow deviation from practice without causing a bit of a fuss, and therefore they act to police those responsible for inputting data, of whatever kind, by refusing to accept anything outside the design parameters. This raises issues of academic and professional freedom, power and control. This is not really an IT issue at all, since such constraints result from CBMS *per se* not the use of the computer. However, neither the IT system nor CBMS determines levels of access. This is a matter for management: the degree of access says something about the philosophy of the system and through this of those who manage the institution.

One of the major dilemmas for any institution is how to acquire the right IT system and software. There are basically two approaches. Either you develop it yourself or you 'buy in'. Both approaches have their benefits and drawbacks. There are some very good commercial packages available on the market to support all or some of the systems underpinning CBMS wherever they reside on the curriculum continuum. The major drawback of this is that they have not been designed with a particular university's specific scheme in mind. Often they aim at a generic CBMS model which does not in reality exist, or they have developed from a specific model and are then generalized to meet a wider market. Either way they need to be adapted by the institution and this can allow bugs to get into the system. Alternatively, the CBMS framework needs to be adapted to suit the computer program. There is, however, nothing worse for academics to be told that the reason they cannot do something is that the computer will not allow it. This is a common response from IT managers and serves to undermine the true value of CBMS and of IT. The response must be that the computer does not allow it because the CBMS framework which it serves, and which is developed by the academic community, does not allow it for sound educational reasons.

### *IT and Staff*

This emphasizes a second problem and that is that the IT systems are usually designed by technocrats rather than by those who fully understand curriculum development, and they find it hard to communicate effectively with academics who they might see as being only semi literate in IT terms and therefore unable to understand the real issues! Of course, the academics take the reverse view, that it is the technocrats who are curriculum illiterates. Thus dialogue between the two camps is essential in order to prevent entrenchment behind this unhelpful polarization. The problem is that effective dialogue requires the use of a common language and this is rarely easy. There are too few staff well versed in curriculum development and IT development at truly sophisticated levels in both cases. As a sector, HE would do well to acknowledge the need for, and value of, such staff and take positive steps to develop a career pathway within institutions for such individuals, supported by appropriate staff development. It is likely that within the next generation of students there will be those with good IT skills who have been through genuine CBMS experiences themselves who could provide this important resource assuming that it is valued sufficiently.

These problems are not necessarily resolved by developing the IT systems in-house. Whilst programs can be designed to meet specific requirements, they are not necessarily cost effective. To some extent programmers must re-invent wheels and find solutions to *general* CBMS problems. Errors can be expensive both in monetary terms and in terms of undermining confidence in the university's CBMS curriculum. Those not well disposed towards CBMS find IT a useful weapon with which to beat the CBMS enthusiasts. In-house IT technicians are no different from their external counterparts in that they share the objective to develop an effective IT *system* rather than an effective support system for the CBMS *philosophy*. However, for the academic, this technical 'systems' goal is a means to an end. Chalk face academics simply want basic, reliable, accurate information on time. The problem for the technocrat is that university teachers rarely have the ability to identify their needs accurately in advance of the specification that they give to the IT designers. Academics are in any case rarely involved in this discussion, since the system side is rarely seen as having an educational output. Thus the purpose of dialogue ought to be to establish the common goals that the team have in developing CBMS. The IT system does not simply *serve* the CBMS as an adjunct but is just as much an integral part of CBMS design as, say, the assessment scheme or the module choice framework.

IT systems encapsulate the collective CBMS consciousness of the institution because they ought to describe the particular philosophy that the university has adopted. IT encapsulates some basic first principles such as:

- assessment rules;
- module choice regulations;
- timetabling;
- registration and conferment information.

All of this must be described in a standard form irrespective of particular student pathways. On the other hand, such description, and control through the IT system, does not guarantee a *corporate* vision of CBMS, in that there are usually many CBMS dilemmas that remain unresolved in an institution and sometimes also undebated. The IT system reflects a series of compromises or, as the losers in the debate would argue, 'imposed solutions'. Sometimes this mismatch between the collective consciousness embedded in the IT system and the fragmented consciousness embedded in the real world of academic debate serves to undermine the effectiveness of both the CBMS framework and the IT system which is part of it. In a non-CBMS process, where the tutor has greater autonomy, it is possible to vary the assessment methodology, timing of assessments and examinations and pretty much everything else since little needs to be transparent. If the impact of such variation is contained within the systems of one department or faculty and the relevant administrative office, such autonomy remains manageable, if somewhat disempowering for students. Under CBMS much greater coordination is required. Thus if a student is taking modules in French and geology, before the Awards Board can make any decisions about the award for that student it needs marks from both French and geology. It needs that information at a time convenient to the Awards Board and not the French or geology staff! Thus academics are constrained to finish their assessments by a due date. Failure to do so does not just inconvenience students at a course specific level but undermines the whole awards process of the university in a serious way. One disenchanted or inefficient member of staff, or simply one with a cold, can have powerful disrupting consequences unless managed appropriately! The cost of greater flexibility for students is that staff have to work to tighter time lines. If flexibility is important for the future survival of institutions, then it is a cost that most staff are reluctantly willing to pay. On the other hand, where institutions are protected from the harsher side of the educational mass market, flexibility has not developed at a particularly fast rate. There is still a place for tradition in niche marketing!

Similarly, students have to be disciplined in making decisions on time, no bad thing in itself! Thus, for example, before the IT system can timetable students in such a way as to maximize an individual's choice, it needs to know the possible permutations of choice that are required of it by the student body. Neither students nor academic staff necessarily see meeting externally imposed deadlines (by the computer as they see it) as a first priority. Therefore a major cultural change is likely to be required when CBMS is introduced. Similarly, with CBMS there needs to be an agreed system for assessment, for example the use of grades as opposed to percentages (or *vice versa*). This must be built in as part of the regulations. What cannot occur is for the CBMS framework to be based on a grading system and one or two academics or departments to operate on percentages. The computer cannot cope and should not be expected to. The computer is there to generate sound and consistent information for staff and students. The introduction of IT systems to provide effective data analysis may be perceived by some as a 'big brother' policing system, which might appear to run counter to the culture of academic freedom. Whilst we do not endorse conformity as a goal, we would argue that most academic staff welcome, as do students, consistency, continuity and fairness. CBMS exposes inequity across disciplines. The IT system underpinning CBMS helps in this process.

Academics complain about doing administration. However, some seem reluctant to hand it over to those who are best able and trained to deal with it: administrators. 'This is not my job its administration . . . You can't do this you're just an administrator'! CBMS, with its integrated IT systems, threatens these attitudes. As Theodossin (1986, p. 38) points out, the growth of administrative involvement enhances the influence of those administrators and the possibility of their control over academic activity. A common area of dispute is timetabling. The departmental Principal Lecturer who has for a number of years legitimized his or her position in the institution in terms of the important academic task of timetabling is now faced with the possibility of this task being done effectively by a good administrator and a computer in a central office. The focus is now on student choice and the ability of that computer to maximize that choice to meet the needs of the student within the CBMS rules. This raises the issue of who gets access to the all powerful computer and with what purpose. There is a theoretical continuum of access from, at one extreme, where all have 'read and change' access, to the other extreme where such access is controlled by a few. We have said throughout that CBMS requires and provides transparency so that its systems, processes and regulations are clear and public. For an IT system to work to the advantage of a CBMS institution it must also subscribe to this principle. However, just as it is crucial that the IT technicians *serve the curriculum* and do not *drive* it, the academics and administrators must *serve the IT system* in the interests of that curriculum. The difficulty is to get this cultural change understood and embedded in the organization. A partnership is required that is based on transparency of values and processes. CBMS is more than just a system. It is a collection of shared values which should underpin the processes which guide *inter alia* the IT systems. The issues of ownership and control of the system need to be openly debated and a sensible policy on systems access, based upon clarity of purpose, developed from this. IT staff need to feel confident that in making the system serve the institution, by being genuinely accessible and user friendly, they are consolidating rather than jeopardizing their jobs. Supporting *all* staff across the university, by ensuring that they have the right level of access to do their respective jobs effectively, must be a priority. In CBMS, access to the IT system at various levels is invariably in the hands of administrative staff (sometimes at a relatively low level in the hierarchy) rather than academics. The reason for restricting access is not, as is sometimes claimed, because of issues of confidentiality but that the more open the access the greater the chance of error and confusion. Access levels must therefore be based on a functional analysis of job requirement and not status or self-perceived status. They are also based on trust. It must be assumed that those with access to the system (the administrators) at various levels, can be trusted to do the job properly for those who do not (academics). Access to the IT system, of course, empowers. It empowers differentially according to levels of access and this can be a cause of tension.

### IT and Students

One group that the system can empower more than most is students. Given appropriate access rights and provided the IT system is designed with students, as well as staff in mind, the IT system can free staff of a great deal of traditional work mediating between the student and the curriculum and allow students access to information which allows them to make genuine choices on matters such as:

- the nature of modules;
- the nature of assessment;
- the timetable for the module;
- who teaches the module.

Information transparency has been accepted in the context of library catalogues, where students are encouraged to search freely for factual information. This is seen both as an acceptable and liberating role for students. With a student-focused IT system for CBMS, much the same can be achieved. Thus they can choose their own pattern of work, and possibly style of learning, by selecting modules which suit *their* timetable requirements or learning needs. It may help them with domestic requirements or employment needs. In the context of the developing mass education system in the UK, with students depending less and less on state finances, this is becoming an important consideration for many students. We believe that a curriculum management and IT system which has transparency as a goal is central to any consideration of CBMS. The transparent IT-based process also opens the curriculum up to prospective students world-wide with access through the world wide web. It can be used as a marketing tool through the internet in the same way as library catalogues are now global.

Whilst students may remain in need of sound advice from staff, the advice relationship changes fundamentally. Students are no longer dependant upon individual members of staff to provide factual information as well as judgments. Through an effective and transparent IT system students have access to sound and secure factual information about module provision. In approaching staff they come armed with a battery of information. They also therefore have the ability to test out the efficacy of the member of staff's own level of understanding and therefore judgment! This is, of course, a threat for some staff. However, making judgments on sound information is superior to maintaining judgments of variable quality that may be person dependent, however helpful the person wishes to be. This process also frees time for academics and others to focus on other important aspects of their jobs, such as teaching and research.

We have so far talked about the input side of the information equation, which provides students with information about how to make the best choices about their programmes of study and working patterns either with or without the support of an adviser. An effective IT system also provides output information which enables staff, students and prospective employers with information with which to make judgments. Within CBMS the assumption is that credit accumulation will lead to, and build up, information on student progress over a period of time so the student and adviser can see the attainment of the student as the pathway unfolds. This provides an insight into individual strengths and weaknesses, that *the student* can use to determine future action including changes to the programme of study (again with or without guidance from staff). This allows students to determine their own strategy with regard to the nature of the award to be achieved. Thus if the student knows the basis for degree classification and knows progress to date, it is possible for the student to determine how best to achieve the goals set by himself or herself and how to manipulate the situation to the best advantage. Again, many academics find this uncomfortable, since the assessment regime and especially the final decision about the class of degree have previously been nothing to do with the student. It was the ultimate point at which staff demonstrated their control of the teaching and learning relationship.

This process of gradually building up the achievement profile of the student also allows, through effective IT, for the development and production of transcripts. In other words the student and prospective employer can receive more than just information about the name of the award and class of degree achieved, but also an insight into the complete range of the student's achievement over his or her HE career. This can subsequently be used as a more sophisticated means of allowing students to develop graduate profiles which some institutions believe takes the transcript to the next logical stage of development by listing extra curricular activity and the attainment of key skills. Transcripts can range from the very basic (a list of modules taken and passed) through to those which genuinely reflect the nature of the data available on the IT system. This could include AP(E)L data, fail marks as well as passes, compensation and referrals. The transcript, therefore, can take on a very significant role. It gives employers genuine information that perhaps the student may be less keen on displaying. This is of course not a good reason for keeping employers in the dark! It again challenges however, the taken for granted assumptions of many academics and students who prefer to retain the 'mystery' of the degree. The transcript can become a barometer of the sophistication of the CBMS system and an indication of the extent to which the system reflects a culture of credit rather than of just awards. Transcripts give detail of learning achieved. They emphasize learning ladders and life-long learning. They give an indication of the sophisticated path that HE will need to travel in meeting the needs of employers in the 21st century. Unfortunately, many employers brought up under the old regime are not sufficiently aware of this need themselves and there will remain a danger that transcripts will be misunderstood to the detriment of the students and the institutions that introduce them. But CBMS institutions are used to blazing such trails and it is encouraging to see that there is beginning to develop a national recognition of this important development (HEQC, 1997b; Dearing, 1997). The institutions themselves will have to play a key role in explaining to employers how such transparency is likely to benefit them.

Finally, however effective the IT system, it cannot and should not be considered infallible. We know of one particular case, where the first live run through of a two tiered assessment process had gone badly wrong due to ineffective IT. Software had failed to deliver and hardware had under performed. The institution could not afford a second failure and considerable resources were devoted to getting it right the second time around. Systems were tested and found to be effective and systems managers were confident that the IT would perform up to specification. This it did, much to the relief of institutional managers, until lightning struck (literally) at a key point in the process and blew out the lines supporting data transfer. The gods have a sense of humour.

### Resourcing and Planning

One of the dilemmas facing any curriculum framework is how best to organize its resourcing. This is not the same question as where to find the resources in the first place, important as this is. Staff are keen to know how institutional managers will resource the delivery of programmes of study where flexibility brings instability in planning. Managers need to consider how best to distribute limited resources around the CBMS institution in such a way that it contributes to effective delivery. It is effective IT systems which in part help managers solve this problem. One of the major difficulties with resourcing in a flexible CBMS model is how to ensure that the resources track through to the point of delivery when they are actually needed. Under a traditional model, the department aims to recruit a specific number of students either to hit a predetermined target for which monies will be allocated or in order to justify an historically derived budget. Resource allocators will have a rough idea, or even an exact idea, of the resources required in that particular area. However, in CBMS, students are given a high degree of choice over which modules they select and they do not necessarily do this in advance of departmental budget allocations as they would under a traditional curriculum model. Students may be choosing only a term or semester ahead. Indeed, first year students may not give any true indication until they enter the portals of the university for the first time. Second and subsequent years students can be requested or required to predict likely programmes of study for the future but choice implies realistic choice and therefore the possibility of changing minds. This means that resource allocators at every level in the institution may get surprises. A well recruiting module in one year may fail to attract the next year. This is not a major difficulty because resources can be redistributed. The problem is the speed at which this is done, especially for the module which recruits above expectation and is found to be seriously under resourced suddenly. This becomes very apparent where resource issues like staffing and accommodation are concerned. To discover suddenly a demand from 50 students for a module allocated to a room designed for 20 causes embarrassment and anger if it is not identified rapidly. Similarly, where a popular module needs to be run on a number of occasions in a week or term, there will be additional inputs required from staff while less popular modules run with lower staff student ratios. Under traditional curriculum frameworks such difficulties can be hidden for as long as politically expedient by manipulating the demand for a pro-gramme. In CBMS the problem becomes immediate. Short term initiatives are introduced to overcome the problem by, for example, putting limits on the number of students allowed on a module. But this causes other difficulties relating to the criteria used to disallow recruitment to the module. Usually this leads to a highly contested list such as:

- first come first served; this of course then has to be modified because some students require the module as a compulsory part of their programme;
- compulsory students first followed by optional students next (but then you need to determine on what basis you distinguish between optional students — first come first served?)

Such processes also discriminate against 'in-fill' or associate students who wish simply to take a specific module rather than a complete award. Some of these may be part-time students who are sponsored by their company at very profitable rates. In a traditionally-based institution these problems are minimized by the planning controls in place to restrict access to particular funded target levels. Students register on courses which have targets. Courses are taught by departments containing staff. Therefore the distribution of the income is based on the fees brought into the department by the student plus additional monies available to the institution through, for example, the funding bodies, again distributed on a formula basis around student numbers in the department. There may of course be squabbles over the formula or whatever mechanism the institution may operate to distribute monies to departments, but the process is relatively simple. The more students the more money to teach them. However, CBMS creates difficulties for this simple regime because, once the system moves along the continuum towards greater flexibility, students begin to break out of the departmental barriers and therefore cross the departmental budgetary lines as well. Combined Studies students may be taking credits within the department of History and the department of Sociology from completely different faculties and therefore budgets. Negotiated students may be taking modules from as many departments across the university as there are modules in their programmes.

Clearly, it is not appropriate to allocate arbitrarily a student to the department where most of the programme is taught and hope that a swings and roundabout process will even things out. It is important to have an IT system that tracks the student at the level of the module taken. If this is in place, it becomes possible to develop a *credit-based funding process* rather than a student-based process. Under such a regime, monies follow the student *credits* delivered by a department rather than students *per se*. Thus if a student takes the bulk of his or her studies in the department of History the bulk of the money will track through to it. The balance will go to the Sociology department and Business Studies or whatever. Clearly, this requires a management information system (MIS) that is effective in tracking the distribution of resources that a student attracts. Hitherto, in many institutions the financial IT systems have not been appropriately integrated to any degree of sophistication. The IT software which tracks the student's academic programme for the purposes of academic information, counselling and for ensuring that the programme fits the rules, must also interface effectively with the budgetary and finance programmes in the institution. Resource provision and the curriculum become integrated, at the very least, at the level of sharing information and there must be a very good case now for shared development of these aspects of MIS. It would be of great advantage to an institution to be able to call up on the IT system a student's number and get information simultaneously on the student's academic and resource profiles. Such levels of information allow managers to undertake much more sophisticated levels of planning at institutional level because they make clear to all members of the institution that students really are very directly the unit of resource for the institution.

A credit-based system of resourcing within an institution running CBMS becomes of particular significance, and provides major benefits, in those areas where parts of the curriculum are delivered or offered externally, such as to companies (see Chapter 5). Modules as discrete units of academic credit can be developed for this market as full cost provision (provision in which the full costs, including profits, are charged to the recipient directly rather than mediated through funding body grants). This has planning benefits for the providers and also offers transparent and user friendly information to the customers. The way in which a credit-resourced curriculum allows for a 'learn and pay by instalment approach' offers a strong incentive to company sponsors who may wish to spread the cost of an investment in the education and training of employees over several financial years. In a traditional curriculum model it is difficult or impossible to disaggregate an award in this way, either academically or financially. The common response to this is to design special short courses with all the development costs that this entails. Short courses of this nature do not fit seamlessly into an existing award structure and would require special processes of credit recognition through APL (see Chapter 6). CBMS facilitates a different approach to the professional development of people in work in any case. Credit-rated modules may focus on a particular training need of a company such as say accounting or marketing, and not be seen necessarily as part of a degree, at least not at first. The fact that CBMS allows for credit to be both a transportable free standing achievement and part of a progression path to a complete award that may be accessed at the convenience of the student, provides a strong incentive to employers and employees to join such programmes. CBMS meets particular needs and allows focused costing and flexible payment.

Effective IT supports CBMS in providing a basis for sophisticated planning strategies, in comparison with the traditional curriculum, especially in regard to the recruitment of students. Curriculum planning and development can be fast, but more importantly, it can be piecemeal. There is no need to develop a complete three year degree in, say, cryogenics just because there appears to be a new market opening up. The possibility of combined studies programmes offering 'half' subjects or, indeed, a series of modules as part of a more flexible programme approach allows an institution to test the market and retain or recruit staff. CBMS also allows the introduction of a new area of study without necessarily undermining a related but less popular area which could have dire consequences on staff through redundancy. Thus, for example, an institution faced with a decline in numbers to its single honours sociology degree programme might introduce psychology as a 'half' subject which can be combined with sociology. Whilst a full psychology degree might have been possible, this may have caused the sociology to decline further. However, the popular psychology could bring about a rise in sociology numbers by being offered as an attractive combination, thus allowing the sociology department to take stock and reposition itself for the future. Effective modelling, based on the manipulation of data contained within an integrated IT system, becomes feasible. This illustrates a major shift in curriculum planning away from the departmental base to a higher level, where strategic decisions can be taken. Left to their own devices, as is possible and common in traditional curriculum institutions, the Psychology department could undermine the Sociology department without really trying! Strategically planned, both departments can prosper.

*Chapter 9*

# Higher Education in the Learning Society: Issues for Credit-based Modular Systems

'Higher Education in the Learning Society', the Report of the National Committee chaired by Sir Ron Dearing, was published in July 1997 (Dearing, 1997) and was a long awaited inquiry into the state of HE in the UK. It was the first such inquiry since the Robbins report published in 1963 (Robbins, 1963), which is why we give it special prominence here. In our view, the Dearing Report fails to live up to the expectations that many had of it. Dearing presents a broad vision of the future of HE in a learning society to which many in the sector and government would subscribe (DfEE, 1998a, 1998b). CBMS provides a platform for meeting many of the Dearing recommendations quickly and positively. However, the devil is in the detail and Dearing fails on many fronts to provide clarity, or to propose action, and therefore he fails to move the debate on curriculum design and management forward in the way many hoped he would.

Thus he says:

> We address the principle in our terms of reference: that *'Learning should be increasingly responsive to employment needs and include the development of general skills, widely valued in employment'*. In doing so, we have had in mind the need to build on the established strengths of higher education. (Dearing, 1997, p. 130)

We would argue that 'established strengths' is a contested concept which Dearing fails to address. Instead he attempts to reconcile or treat as uniform the very different philosophies which drive HE in the late 20th century. We have admitted to a wholehearted endorsement of the CBMS framework for the future and there are hints in Dearing that this framework has an important role to play in that future. However, Dearing has not taken development any further, instead he has encouraged compromise and this has led to confusion and to our way of thinking is retrograde in its effect on CBMS.

Unlike the Kennedy Report on Further Education (FE) (Kennedy, 1997), which takes a clear and uncompromising position, Dearing provides a prime example of how compromise fails to produce clarity especially when in the context of CBMS. As we have shown, CBMS has exposed many academic fudges and this is in the long term good for higher education. Dearing has sought to do what CBMS has sought to avoid, that is produce all the flexibilities and advantages to students and industry through the creation of a more vision-ary curriculum but without upsetting the apple cart of the traditionalists. We feel that the best approach to an analysis of Dearing is to take those of his recommendations which impinge directly upon the development of CBMS and see where it takes the current debate. We will not focus on all of the recom-mendations, although many relating to widening access could be seen to be met more effectively through CBMS.

Recommendation 1
We recommend to the Government that it should have a long term strategic aim of responding to increased demand for higher education, much of which we expect to be at sub-degree level, and that to this end, the cap on full-time undergraduate places should be lifted over the next two to three years and the cap on full-time sub-degree places should be lifted immediately.

In the context of this book we do not need to focus on the issue of capping or otherwise, except we would argue that the distinction between full-time and part-time is increasingly problematic in the context of credit-based programmes. The key issue here, in so far as it impinges on CBMS, is Dearing's concept of sub-degree. Sub-degree to Dearing appears to refer to work completed at the levels prior to the level or stage at which graduation is completed, which is meaningless in a credit accumulation system. By sub-degree Dearing means awards like the HND/C as opposed to awards like the BA/BSc. However, what he fails to recognize (and therefore encourage) is that in the context of CBMS the so called sub-degree *award* could be in fact an integral part of a *programme of study* leading to the degree award. In a credit accumulation programme of study, especially one based on modular provi-sion, students could be registered on modules which lead to both the HND/C and the degree. Alternatively, students registered on the different awards could well be sharing modules and gaining credit towards their respective awards. In this sense the modules are not sub-degree at all but at degree level (probably levels 1 and 2). There may be debate about the extent to which HND/C modules should be the same as those leading to a degree, but in many institu-tions this debate has been had and decisions made to produce integrated CBMS programmes. Wherever one stands on this, Dearing confuses the situ-ation rather than clarifies it, by failing to build this more sophisticated approach to award structures and programme design into his thinking. Some might argue that this false distinction between the sub-degree award and the degree programme has been proposed in order to facilitate development of levels 1 and 2 of degree programmes in FE institutions, where costs are less and there-fore standards different. Dearing reinforces this by later stating that year 3 should not be franchised by universities to FE institutions, thus implying that the standards for Years 1 and 2 and the resources devoted to Years 1 and 2 in FE Colleges (as opposed to first and second year students in the universities) can be lower. He can, therefore, have his cake and eat it by claiming to maintain university standards and widen access.

Recommendation 2
We recommend to Government and the Funding Bodies that, when allocating funds for the expansion of higher education, they give priority to those institutions which can demonstrate a commitment to widening participation, and have in place a participation strategy, a mechanism for monitoring progress, and provision for review by the governing body of achievement.

We welcome this recommendation in the belief that those institutions based on CBMS philosophies have been in a better position to respond to this requirement, since credit and modularism facilitate both franchising in a wider geographical context, and a wider range of methods of entry via AP(E)L. They also facilitate progression and transfer. If the transparency of CBMS is properly managed, it is likely to have an appeal to a wide section of the community. A learning experience defined in terms of learning outcomes is more likely to be meaningful and appear relevant than one defined simply by curriculum content. Widening participation is not just about numbers but is also about widening access for more diverse groups in the context of increasing age participation rates. For those for whom participation in HE is likely to be focused on personal achievement linked to professional or career progression, the transparency of CBMS is likely to have greater attraction.

Recommendation 8
We recommend that, with immediate effect all institutions of higher education give high priority to developing and implementing learning and teaching strategies which focus on the promotion of students' learning.

We would endorse this recommendation from Dearing, but would wish to take it further. Dearing is essentially arguing for good teaching and good teachers with students at the centre of the learning process. Few could object to that. Dearing stresses the need for:

wider support and guidance for students which enables them to focus their attention fully on their learning. We believe that the achievement of our vision will establish the United Kingdom (UK) as a leader in the world of learning and teaching at higher levels. In our view this must be a national objective. (Dearing, 1997, p. 114)

However, putting the student at the centre of the learning process means more than dynamic and facilitative teaching and learning processes. It means putting students' needs at the heart of the curriculum and the design of their programmes of study. The flexibility, transparency and choice offered by CBMS provide this in a way that traditionally developed curricula do not. Many critics of CBMS have pointed to the fragmented nature of flexible modular experiences. Dearing is right to stress the need for high quality guidance to ensure that diversity in meeting needs is not fragmentation through lack of focus.

> Recommendation 9
> We recommend that all institutions should, over the medium term, review the changing role of staff as a result of communications and information techno-logy, and ensure that staff and students receive appropriate training and sup-port to enable them to realise its full potential.

This is fundamental to successful CBMS development and delivery. As we have indicated elsewhere CBMS is based on the assumption that staff and students have access to, and know how to interrogate successfully, databases which facilitate the management of and choice in flexible and sometimes complex modular systems. The aims of CBMS are more likely to be met if staff and students have access to hardware and the skills to use the software.

> Recommendation 11
> We recommend that: institutions of higher education, over the medium term, integrate their careers services more fully into academic affairs and that the provision of careers education and guidance is reviewed periodically by the Quality Assurance Agency; (and that) the Government, in the medium to long term should integrate careers advice for life long learning, to complement services based inside higher education institutions.

We would not wish to claim that CBMS is special in respect of this recom-mendation. Good careers advice is important whatever the curriculum model adopted. However, we would argue that in the context of CBMS careers advice should not be seen as something which is optional and which comes towards the end of a programme when the student begins to contemplate the future world of employment. The flexibility of CBMS makes it essential that career planning is run in parallel with individual curriculum programme planning for all students. We would also argue, however, that CBMS provides opportunities for such planning to be an integral part of the curriculum itself through the credit-based modular programme via, for example, the use of profiling mod-ules and work-based modules.

> Recommendation 16
> We recommend that all institutions of higher education, over the medium term, review the programmes they offer: with a view to securing a better balance between breadth and depth across programmes than currently exists; so that all undergraduate programmes include sufficient breadth to enable specialists to understand their specialism within its context.

We applaud this recommendation and recognize it as something which is achievable within CBMS. However, what is regrettable is that Dearing does not in his report make the same link. This recommendation illustrates Dearing's attempt to be forward looking yet not step on too many toes by pushing against traditional models of the curriculum too much. It is this attempt to be all things to all people which undermines his later recommendations for a qualifications framework. Within CBMS it is possible for students to select modules which provide an in-depth single subject focus alone. Alternatively, it is possible to guide, or compel the student through regulation, to select a modular pattern which provides a wider context for that single subject approach. It is possible to do this in the early years of study or throughout. However, it is important to make such broadening content an integral part of the main programme, in order to signal its importance and provide motivation to students.

Recommendation 18
We recommend that all institutions should, over the medium term, identify opportunities to increase the extent to which programmes help students to become familiar with work, and help them to reflect on such experience.

Similarly, we would argue that CBMS institutions are in a strong position to respond to this initiative. Modules which focus on the world of work can be readily integrated into a student's programme without a major re-design of that programme of the type that will be required in traditional models unless such provision is to be treated as an additional 'bolt on'. Thus in the CBMS curriculum students could be required, or given the opportunity, to undertake a single work-based module or a series according to the interpretation of this Dearing recommendation. These can be built into the curriculum plan of the particular student during the guidance and choice processes. In a traditionally designed curriculum extensive redesign work will be required to meet this need.

Recommendation 20
We recommend that institutions of higher education, over the medium term, develop a progress file. The file should consist of two elements: a transcript recording student achievement which should follow a common format devised by institutions collectively through their representative bodies; a means by which students can monitor, build and reflect upon their personal development.

Here again, we can see that Dearing is developing themes that are established features of CBMS. In developing the latter, institutions have had to confront the issues which Dearing has brought to the fore. Thus issues of transcripts, profiles, records of achievement and the like have been developed as an integral part of many CBMS programmes. The reason for this is that CBMS has demanded a level of transparency hitherto not an essential feature of the higher education sector. Thus, for example, if a student is taking a flexible credit-based modular degree the transcript is an important database describing and recording the student's programme and achievement within it.

It is disappointing that Dearing continually fails to give CBMS higher visibility in his report.

> Recommendation 21
> We recommend that institutions of higher education begin immediately to develop, for each programme they offer, a 'programme specification' which identifies potential stopping off points and gives the intended outcomes of the programme in terms of: the knowledge and understanding that a student will be expected to have on completion; key skills . . . cognitive skills . . . [and] subject specific skills.

Again, Dearing is advocating at a level of detail for higher education in general much that is embedded in the practice of CBMS institutions. Although other non-CBMS institutions could well be approaching these issues, some are integral to the credit-based curriculum and therefore cannot be avoided. Thus transparency via 'programme specification' is essential to the credit-based process of progression through stages or to put it in Dearing's negative way, 'stopping-off point'. Such progression is based upon a clear award framework with interim points and awards building to an end award.

> Recommendation 22
> We recommend that the Government, representative bodies, the Quality Assurance Agency, other awarding bodies and the organisations which oversee them, should endorse immediately the framework for higher education qualifications that we have proposed.

It is most unlikely that these bodies will endorse Dearing's framework. This recommendation is deeply disappointing given that earlier recommendations above point to Dearing's wider understanding of some of the principles underlying CBMS. We believe that Dearing has, through his framework, attempted to meet the needs of all the traditions of the UK, and as such has demonstrated a lack of understanding of just how far part of the HE sector has already gone in developing such frameworks. Even if Dearing had accepted the existing CNAA CATS model (CNAA, 1989), more progress would have been made. Instead Dearing treads his own path (as if unaware that experts have been through the jungle prior to him) and thus takes us in the wrong direction. Given the significance of this recommendation for the subject of this book we will review it in some detail.

Dearing proposes a framework based on four undergraduate levels (see Figure 9.1).

The Dearing dilemma does not arise from his framework of four undergraduate levels *per se* because as we have shown in Chapter 3 theoretically any number of levels is possible provided they are based on an internally consistent and transparent approach. Dearing however demonstrates the traps that many fall into when he illustrates the application of his framework in Figure 9.2.

*Figure 9.1: A qualification framework*

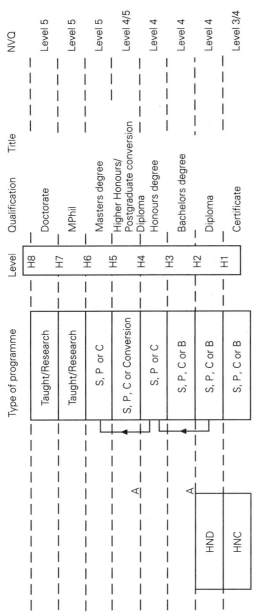

| Type of programme | Level | Qualification | Title | NVQ |
|---|---|---|---|---|
| Taught/Research | H8 | Doctorate | | Level 5 |
| Taught/Research | H7 | MPhil | | Level 5 |
| S, P or C | H6 | Masters degree | | Level 5 |
| S, P, C or Conversion | H5 | Higher Honours/ Postgraduate conversion | | Level 4/5 |
| S, P or C | H4 | Diploma Honours degree | | Level 4 |
| S, P, C or B | H3 | Bachelors degree | | Level 4 |
| S, P, C or B | H2 | Diploma | | Level 4 |
| S, P, C or B | H1 | Certificate | | Level 3/4 |

HND

HNC

A level/GNVQ/Access

Type of programme
A = Accelerated route if correct number of specialist credit points acquired
S = Single subject
C = Combined subjects
B = Broad range of subjects
P = Subject leading to professional status
Conversion = postgraduate conversion course

Note
1. Each level up to H4 would require at least 120 additional credit points.
2. Students pursuing broad programmes at levels H1.H2 and H3 and securing 360 credit points would be awarded a Bachelors degree.
3. To achieve an Honours degree would require at least 360 specialist credit points. The rate of progress would depend on the amount of previous specialisation.
4. It would be for each institution, consulting as appropriate with the professional bodies to determine the pattern of credits (e.g. how much specialisation or how much breadth) required to qualify for an Honours degree.

*Source:* HMSO, 1997

135

*Figure 9.2: Examples of routes through the framework*

Student A had always been interested in English and wanted to study it in depth in higher education. Having acquired the relevant A levels, she entered higher education as a full-time student and followed the single subject route and left with an Honours degree at level H4. She takes no breaks and completes her Honours degree in three years by the accelerated route.

Student B was interested in science, but less sure about the specific area she wanted to study. She entered higher education and studied a General Sciences programme up to level H2 on a full-time basis. She left full-time studies with a diploma having got a job as a technician in a laboratory. She continued her studies on a part-time basis sponsored by her employer focusing on biology and acquired an Honours degree at level H4.

Student C, following a Short Service Commission in the Army, wanted to retrain as a primary school teacher, specialising in education of young children. He enrolled on a BEd programme which enabled him to study for a profession and acquire a range of subject knowledge. He left with an Honours degree at level H4. Later, in order to progress in his career and update his skills, he enrolled on a part-time MEd programme. This took him up to level H6.

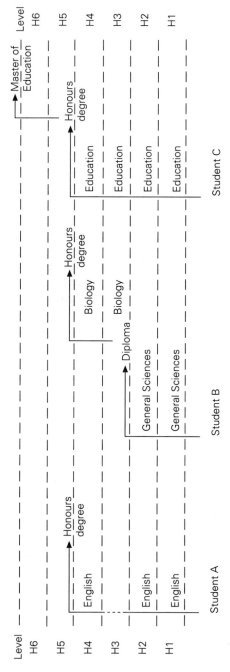

*Source:* HMSO, 1997

Dearing's *qualifications* framework is just that. A framework of qualifications and not a *credit* framework. As such, his report takes the HE sector backwards rather than along the visionary road he outlines in the early chapters of his report. Seamless progression through levels cannot be based on the deconstructivist approach (i.e. simply deconstructing traditional models to fit a new framework). In our view, progression through levels can only be based upon a transparent system of credit accumulation in which key criteria, such as the definition of levels and outcomes in terms of standards of attainment and the volume of credit within each level, are well defined and consistent.

Dearing's difficulties are illustrated by his example of student A. Here he retains (for reasons that are not difficult to surmise) the picture of the three year honours student taking a single subject traditional degree, common in many UK institutions and which it would be politically difficult to undermine. Thus Dearing needs to show that this model can be retained in a framework which assumes progression through stages but which baulks at making explicit the credits gained and the levels passed through. Dearing therefore has to call this student's programme an 'accelerated route'. But whereas other accelerated programmes (HEFCE, 1996) define the outcomes, levels and credits in precisely the same terms as non-accelerated routes (e.g. 360 credits at levels 1, 2 and 3) and acceleration occurs by APL/APEL and heavier timetables (teaching through summer), Dearing just misses a complete stage out (H3)! So much for standards. His rationale appears to be that this is a single subject area studied by a good student. So much for his encouragement of breadth in degree work!

In our view, Dearing's qualifications framework leaves many questions unanswered. Despite saying that 'progress should depend on aptitude . . . and the credits acquired' (p. 152), there is no further attempt to link volume of credit to the various levels of his framework. To practitioners, or would-be practitioners, of CBMS this will not make any sense although, ironically, it may be less challenging for those in traditional systems. Dearing's framework appears to confuse the concepts of level and volume which are essential to the internal logic of CBMS. There is no attempt to define each level in terms of the volume (amount) of credit it contains or the standard of attainment that might be expected or must be achieved within it. Thus the examples given of progression raise many questions. Is the accelerated route of Dearing's Student A what we would hitherto have called a standard full-time route, contained in three years' study as we surmise above? Does the 'do not take H3, go directly to H4' approach imply progression to a higher level or just to Year 3? Does missing H3 mean the accumulation of less credits than students B and C, implying that 'an Honours degree at level H4' might contain either 360 or 480 credits? Does the accelerated route, by missing H3, imply accelerated progression to H4 that subsumes H3 in both learning and credit terms? Is Student A's accelerated route a depth model, Student B's a breadth model and Student C's a practice (vocational) model? By avoiding any reference to level descriptors and credit volumes Dearing makes none of this clear.

There are other recommendations in subsequent chapters of the Dearing report which although not as central to the CBMS issues that we cover in this book are nevertheless indirectly pertinent. These include recommendations 30 and 38 dealing with the needs for links between higher education and industry, recommendation 40 concerning innovative programme design and recommendation 72 which advocates that funding should follow students. Of course, we would not argue that CBMS has automatically solved all of these issues but we believe that the flexibility that underpins CBMS and the transparency of the approaches taken enables institutions to respond rapidly and appropriately to the needs of industry and the professions in a way that maintains the integrity of the curriculum approach. It would be helpful however, if funding regimes reflected the approach developed within CBMS institutions.

External bodies, be they governmental, quality or funding, are often focused on traditional approaches which then need to be adapted to meet CBMS requirements. It is perhaps time to recognize that CBMS is a major player in HE and that the approaches of external agencies should reflect this. Of course, whilst Dearing has been an interesting and important interlude in the development of HE, it is the Green Paper, 'The Learning Age: a renaissance for a new Britain' (DfEE, 1998a) and the government's response to Dearing (DfEE, 1998b) and to Kennedy (DfEE, 1998c) which will set the scene for HE into the next millennium.

*Appendix*

# Case Studies in Credit-based Modular Systems

# Undergraduate Negotiated Programmes

This study shows CBMS in action. The negotiated programme selected here is based on a real case that illustrates how flexible awards can be constructed around the needs of individual students, whilst retaining all the quality assurance checks and balances that would be expected of a conventional programme. Not all negotiated programmes will be as complex as the example given here. Many will accommodate a more straightforward change in direction in terms of award content that cannot be provided within existing provision.

## Background

Carol Jones is a 38-year-old married woman with two children. Having completed her schooling at 16 she undertook various jobs prior to getting married. Once her children were at school themselves Carol, at the age of 27, became an office assistant at a local electronics firm and then a secretary, having developed her word-processing skills at the local Further Education College. Whilst at work, she and her husband bought a local newsagents and retail outlet which Carol joined full-time after three years with the electronics firm. As well as serving in the shop, Carol was responsible for the accounts. She went back to the FE College and undertook evening courses in 'Small Business Management' and 'Accountancy'. She also undertook a three day course on VAT. Carol enjoyed this work at the FE College so much that she decided to take an 'A' level in English. After six years, the couple decided to get out of the retail trade. The husband found employment with a local food manufacturer whilst Carol decided to become a teacher, and approached a local university.

## Entering HE

With one 'A' level, Mathematics and English GCSEs and being a mature student with experience of children, Carol was admitted to the University for a BEd(Hons) Secondary, specializing in English. She did well on the course and enjoyed the academic study and the brief observational sessions in schools. However, following the six week supervised School Experience Carol decided that school teaching was not for her!

She went along to her tutor who said she would support her as best she could in any efforts to transfer to another course since she had done well on the assessment so far and encouraged her to complete the first year. This Carol did, but meantime spoke to Student Services. Unfortunately, the prospect for transfer turned out to be bleak. Carol's main problem was finance. Although she had planned to undertake a four year BEd programme, the year on the course had put a strain on the family finances and Carol and her husband could not contemplate her starting all over again and doing three more years. If anything she needed to get back into employment as quickly as possible.

At first she hoped that she could transfer onto the second year of the English degree. However, when she approached the admissions tutor for English he explained that she had not done enough 'proper' English! Much of her first year had been taken up with Education Studies and part of the English course had been pedagogic in nature. English studies represented only a small proportion of her work on the BEd and this did not cover the same ground as the first year English programme at the University.

### Transferring

However, undeterred Carol spoke to a friend she had made on the staff of the local FE College. Her advice was to approach the other local university which had in place a credit-based modular curriculum. The friend had contacts within the University because of the franchise arrangements that existed between the FE College and the University. The College was running the first two years of the BA(Hons) Business Administration (BABA), to HND and Diploma in Higher Education level. Students undertaking the first two years of BABA transferred to the University for Year 3.

Carol approached the University in late May and was put in touch with the admissions tutor for English. Unfortunately she gave the same view as her counterpart at the other university. A transfer without loss of time would be impossible. There was, however, still a chance. Carol was referred to the Student Adviser for Negotiated Awards. She felt that she was now in a position that might just help her meet her ambition of getting a degree, in a subject she enjoyed studying and within the revised time scale that her family could afford. But a great deal of further discussion was necessary before that successful outcome could be achieved.

### Meeting Students' Needs

The Student Adviser for Negotiated Awards explained that the credit-based modular curriculum had been put in place so that the University could meet the needs of the student. The point was that the University did not expect the student to meet the needs of the University (the traditional approach in HE). The flexible curriculum enabled students to identify courses that best suited their objectives, whether these were purely academic, employment-related or whatever. However, the student would have to realize that traditional academic standards criteria apply and that the student would need to demonstrate that any programme that was constructed met these criteria.

The first task was to identify the background that might be pertinent to future study. From this Carol identified the successful first year she had undertaken on the BEd. In essence this comprised elements of Education Studies, English, and Classroom Observation and Practice. All of this had been assessed through a combination of essays, examinations, a logbook and through tutor observation. The Student Adviser for Negotiated Awards explained that this, as a whole, was equivalent to 120 credits at level 1. But these were general credits and their actual worth would depend on the course that Carol eventually undertook.

The Student Adviser for Negotiated Awards reminded Carol of her other educational experiences. Carol had no other nationally recognized qualifications after 'A' Level but she did have three Certificates from the local FE College. The first and second in 'Small Business Management' and 'Accountancy' had been assessed. The third on VAT had not, but she did have a Certificate of Attendance. Again the Student Adviser for Negotiated Awards reminded Carol that she had a wealth of experience in running a business with her husband and it was possible that some of this might be relevant to any future course. It was clear from the way the discussion was going that if Carol so wished, a degree programme which contained some elements of business studies might be appropriate. Carol confirmed that this was something that would interest her, but she had also enjoyed the English she had done at the other university. The next stage, it was explained was for Carol to look at the University's module catalogue mounted on the World Wide Web, especially focusing on the English and Business programmes. Meanwhile the Credit Evaluator at the University was asked to give a preliminary comment on the three courses undertaken at the FE College. Because the College was local it was possible to do this fairly quickly. Syllabuses were forwarded and a tutor within the University was asked to comment on them in relation to any of the modules available in the Business School. He confirmed that the level of study, in the case of 'Small Business Management' and 'Accountancy' was level 1 but the VAT course was difficult to assess. He confirmed however that 'Small Business Management' covered the learning outcomes (and a few more) of the University Level 1 module 'An Introduction to Small Business Enterprises'. The accountancy course appeared to be very specialist and to cover the introductory ground in a level 1 module for the accountancy degree, 'Basic Accountancy Principles'.

Carol returned for a second interview with the Student Adviser for Negotiated Awards. She felt that some of the early business studies modules in the Business Studies degree were fairly straightforward and she believed that her experience of running the shop and 'doing the books' had put her in a good position to demonstrate that she had the knowledge and skills to cover at least two of them without further study. The Student Adviser for Negotiated Awards agreed therefore that Carol should enrol as soon as possible on the 10 Credit Level 1 APEL module. The aim of the module was to enable Carol to prove to the assessors that her experience had met the specific learning outcomes of these particular modules. The module could be taken via two methods. Either Carol could enrol on a taught APEL Module the following September or undertake the distance learning version. Since Carol was anxious to move the processes along before enrolment in late September she opted for the latter, and proceeded to work through the learning package.

On advice she decided that her Certificate for 'Small Business Management' should go forward officially as APL for which she would claim 10 level 1 Credits against the module 'An Introduction to Small Business Enterprises'. If this was accepted and assuming she successfully completed the APEL distance learning module she would then have a further 10 level 1 credits for the module itself (thus making 20) and any additional credits that she demonstrated she had from her experience against other business studies modules. In the event she made a proposal for a further 50 credits against level 1 modules in the Business Studies degree. Unfortunately, this was not accepted in full and she was given only 40, because the University was not convinced she covered certain of the learning outcomes at sufficient depth.

Whilst this was being undertaken Carol continued her discussions with the Student Adviser for Negotiated Awards. It was decided that with Carol's profile it was unlikely she could gain sufficient credit via APL and APEL to join the Business Studies or Business Administration degree without considerable loss of time and she had already been told that a straight transfer into English was not possible. However, provided she had sufficient appropriate credits available from her studies of English she might be able to enter into the second year of a combined degree in Business Administration and English.

On further examination of the specific credits likely to be available through APL and APEL, against the combined modular programme for Business Administration and English it was likely that Carol would fail on two counts. Firstly the total number of appropriate credits she was likely to achieve was only 100 credits. In the view of the English department, the English taken at her previous university that was relevant was only likely to be equivalent to 30 specific credits. She would be 30 short for a full year's admission with credit. In addition the Business Studies route had certain compulsory modules against which Carol was unable to relate her experience and these according to the Business School were fundamental to the title Business Administration. In other words Carol would not meet the Field rules for Business Administration. English was more flexible as far as compulsory content was concerned. However, Carol simply failed to have credited via her old university course a sufficient number of English Credits. There was nothing in her educational background or life experience that would make up for that. This was a blow.

**Negotiating the Award**

All was not lost however. The Student Adviser for Negotiated Awards explained that the University offered three types of degree programme. The first was the single Honours degree, which although it provided some choice was mainly a single subject degree programme. The second was the combined Honours programme in which two subjects were taken in an equal combination or major/minor. Both these had now been ruled out. Standards have to be maintained and Carol just did not fit the rules to guarantee those standards. The third route was one often used by mature part-time students in work, who have very specific goals which were often work related. They often needed to put together unique combinations of modules to suit their particular work and educational context. Provided Carol had such goals herself and could demonstrate to the satisfaction of the University's Credit Approvals Board that her proposed course had an internal coherence, related to those goals, then she might be able to proceed. She would also need to be sure that her particular proposed combination of modules could be timetabled at least into the near future.

Carol, with the support of the Student Adviser for Negotiated Awards, set about the task of devising a negotiated programme of studies. She decided that as well as Business Administration she had an interest in communication studies and the media. She believed that the work she had undertaken on her BEd in English, and also in the Educational Studies elements, were in part relevant. The University did not itself have a communication studies Field (although it did have Media Studies) so Carol had to set about the task of producing a personal programme of study that the Board would find acceptable as leading to a title which she would propose herself. Carol wished to continue with her Business Administration throughout the rest of her programme so she discussed with her adviser (who liaised with the Business School) which modules might be relevant for her programme. Again with support, she mapped out a programme which contained elements of media studies, sociology and psychology all focusing on her main area of interest, communications. She also proposed that given her approach a further 30 relevant level 1 credits could be identified from her first year BEd programme at the other university. If she convinced the Board of this she would have 120 level 1 credits which would enable her to enter Year 2.

**Practical Problems**

All was going well until Carol and her adviser matched her proposed course against the timetable that the University had in place for the modules. Although centralized timetabling and a cross-university modular system made it easier to identify when modules were to be taught, and although some modification occurred each year to take account of module demand, which might increase the offering of certain popular modules, it was clear that Carol's programme was unworkable. Not on academic grounds (that had still to be tested) but on practical grounds.

One response would have been to change the proposed modules, but Carol's tutor pointed out that the Board would be applying conventional criteria including one of coherence. Simply swapping modules around could undermine the integrity of the award. What is more, one of the modules which clashed was a second year business module which the Business School had insisted was a compulsory element in any respectable business programme. The answer was simple. Carol would enrol on this module, not at the University itself but at the FE College where the first two years of the BABA degree were franchised. This gave her additional timetable slots to utilize. A second module which she desired to do in media studies was unavailable in her second year since it was an option module for the Single and Combined Honours students which had under recruited. The way forward here might have been for Carol to take a distance learning version, but one was not yet available. So it was decided that she would enrol on what staff colloquially referred to as a 'shell' module. In fact this was a self directed learning module in which the learning outcomes and assessment processes are individually negotiated and the student is tutored through the module on an individualized basis. Tutors in media studies agreed to do this in relation to the 'unpopular' module.

### Maintaining Standards

Carol was aware that the work she needed to do to get her APL/APEL and negotiated programme through the system was up to her. The University staff would be supportive but it was her proposal and she had to submit it to the Board. One problem occurred at the Board. Although the external adviser that the University had consulted was largely supportive of the programme as Carol had proposed it, she was concerned about the proposed title, 'Communication and Business Studies'. She felt that this might imply that the student had covered more business studies and what is more with a more conventional content than was merited. This view was reinforced at the Board meeting by Business School representatives. The proposal was agreed but on condition that an appropriate award title could be negotiated with the student. Carol proposed Communication Studies with Business which was accepted, although she felt that the debate the academics had had at the Board meeting was probably the kind of debate that only academics could have!

### The Goal

Carol achieved her goal. She gained a good degree and eventually a job as a researcher at her local radio station. Life on the negotiated programme was anything but dull. Although the University had a good flexible system, the further down the road of flexibility the student travelled the less secure the University processes. For example, prior to entering Year 3, Carol had to negotiate a revision to her agreed programme because staff changes had resulted in amendments to the media studies programme and some of her modules became unavailable. In addition timetables in the Business School were changed at the last minute and they no longer fully dovetailed with the rest of the University. Furthermore the module marks from the FE college came through late (Carol suspects she was forgotten) and this meant that her results were not completed in time for presentation to the second year Examinations Board. However, she felt that the transcript of results that eventually accompanied her degree certificate was instrumental in securing her the job against other candidates with degrees. She was able to give her prospective employer a very detailed account of her educational experience. She also felt that the experience of negotiating her award had given her useful skills that a conventional award might not have done.

# Postgraduate Negotiated Programmes[1]

This case study concerns a senior engineering manager employed by a global manufacturing company with plants at several locations in England. The programme exploits the full flexibility of postgraduate negotiated awards and of the use and design of APEL claims within them. It also illustrates the benefits which the university and the company derive from the negotiation and learning processes.

At the point of entry to the postgraduate negotiated programme at Modcred University, Ken Barnes was Deputy Plant Manager, and had, in effect, reached a glass ceiling as far as further promotion was concerned, due to the company's policy on higher qualifications beyond a certain level. He was an ideal candidate for the negotiated masters programme for a number of reasons. He worked for a company which prided itself on being a learning organization, which nurtured a culture of continuous education and training and which promoted from within wherever possible. Ken had been with the company since school and had gained an HND in Mechanical and Production Engineering as a student apprentice some 18 years previously. He had been on many one, two and three day training courses (in technical and management topics) that were available at the company. The majority of these had been subject to an accreditation exercise by Modcred University a few years earlier and therefore had university credit values. In addition, Ken had attended a number of one and two-week residential courses at various universities. These courses were developed especially for the company and he had subsequently developed and championed their content within the company. Many of the internal courses were delivered by Modcred University, and most of the external courses had been the subject of AP(E)L claims at some time in the past by other candidates from the company. Thus there was mutual trust and confidence between the University and the company, concerning the potential of the people recommended for the programme, and the standing of the in-company activities already achieved. A principal aim of the programme in the context of the company was to maximize those credit-bearing courses that had already been completed, and to maximize the use of APEL, in order to provide a robust yet fast track route for those relatively few senior managers who were at the glass ceiling; and for the University to contribute meaningfully to the major project so as to enhance the project outcomes for the benefit of the company.

Ken's background was such that the University adviser had confidence in accepting him onto the programme and also to agree early on in the development of the programme proposal that he was a suitable candidate for a substantial APEL claim, possibly all of the first two stages (two-thirds of the award). The final stage, the project/dissertation, is a compulsory part of all postgraduate programmes. It is of prime importance in such a work-based programme. Not only must it demonstrate mastery in line with the generic postgraduate outcomes of the University, it must also address the corporate objectives contained in the particular project activity. In some ways, the hardest part for work-based participants is to identify a project of suitable standing and complexity within the company, as a vehicle to demonstrate all these things, at the appropriate time. University rules dictate that the project cannot be something which has already been started before the appointment of an academic supervisor. A project/dissertation title: 'The adaptation of total productive maintenance to western manufacturing plant' was agreed.

Ken was identified by the company on the basis that all the key criteria were met. He was about to begin a project at another plant which it was felt would benefit greatly from the University's involvement. Timescales were such that the development of the APEL claim and the project were begun at the same time.

The APEL development process at Modcred University, although guided by the tutor, is largely self managed. The first stage was to match experiential learning with the learning outcomes and activities associated with the six modules of the University's Certificate in Management amounting to 60 credits. This enabled Ken to demonstrate a solid foundation of general management knowledge and applied skills. In Ken's case, this was achieved by documenting the appropriate application of theoretical knowledge in prior projects, and management roles over the preceding few years. The large number of in-house short courses was not claimed directly, but offered as supporting evidence to the APEL claim, in particular as proof of formal learning of the underpinning knowledge.

The second stage of the APEL claim concentrated on three of the specialist residential courses mentioned above. The three selected areas were chosen because of the direct relevance of the material to the final stage project. Further development of the taught material had been ongoing at the company over the intervening time period, much of it aimed at delivering the material to a wider audience, and embedding the ideas into company philosophy. Thus there was a great deal of high quality material which was available to be used as evidence in the APEL portfolio. There was a further important point regarding this segment of Ken's experience. From the company's point of view, the residential courses he had taken at other universities were crucial in choosing Ken for the project in the first place, because these learning experiences really did make him the ideal man for the job. Therefore it was seen as especially important to both the company and to the University to capture this learning as part of the MSc. These three areas were developed as independent learning modules (shell modules) with the:

- structure of the module;
- development of learning outcomes;
- writing of the commentary;
- selection of evidence;

each being the responsibility of the student in negotiation with his tutor/ adviser. When completed, they formed a particularly strong element of the whole. This section of the claim resulted in three independent learning modules entitled, 'Investment Engineering', 'Precision Engineering', and 'Simplification Engineering'. Following discussion with the company and with his tutor/ adviser Ken proposed the award title, 'MSc (Management of Advanced Engineering Systems)'. This title and the full programme proposal was subsequently approved by the University Credit Approvals Board (UCAB). The written portfolio was supplemented by a *viva voce*, conducted by a panel of academics drawn from the disciplines represented in the portfolio. The main purpose of the *viva* was to discuss in more depth some of the projects and tasks alluded to in the portfolio, in particular to satisfy the panel that the candidate had a full and in-depth grasp of the underpinning theories being deployed.

Meanwhile, the project itself was proceeding very satisfactorily from the University's viewpoint, albeit rather slowly compared to the company norm. However, the plant manager had been fully briefed on the methodology for the project, in relation to the University's requirements, and was fully supportive of the scheme, and the timescales involved. The project task was highly complex, but can be simply expressed as the application of Japanese scheduling and maintenance procedures, and the associated shift patterns, to an existing western plant, with the intention of:

- improving quality;
- improving throughput;
- reducing plant breakdowns and consequent downtime via an improved maintenance regime;
- reducing rework (usually associated with the breakdowns);
- reducing overtime wage bill (usually associated with the rework).

The methodology was to examine each and every facet of the Japanese Production System, analysing why it was included, what the interdependencies were, and what the barriers were/are to its adoption in the British plant. This included benchmarking visits to other plants around the world. Only as a result of this extremely detailed understanding could a new synthesis to suit a western plant be attempted. Installation of new instrumentation, devising new manning levels, job specifications, and retraining a proportion of the workforce went on simultaneously with very high level negotiations with trade unions to ensure that the new regime could be seen to fit within the parameters of the national agreement.

The project was a success from both University and company viewpoints. Such was the thoroughness of research and planning that the whole workforce felt more comfortable with the planned new system, even before it was up and running, than they did with the existing one. However, the main strength of the dissertation was the proof that for something this complex, there is no one solution that is portable across different plants, no matter how elegant or sophisticated it may be; rather it is the methodology which was developed which was to prove to be portable, leading to an individual optimized solution at each and every plant.

The Masters degree was awarded with Distinction. The external examiner took the trouble to write a separate letter commenting that the dissertation was one of the finest pieces of industrial reporting that he had ever read. The project was an outstanding success in company terms, achieving each of the key bullet points by a margin greater than that thought possible at the outset. It was the inherent flexibility of the University's CBMS curriculum, and especially the negotiated postgraduate provision and APEL, that allowed the University to respond so effectively to the needs of a major industrial client.

### Note

1   We are indebted to our colleague Bob Mercer for providing this case study.

# An Approach to AP(E)L

## APL

The accreditation of prior learning (APL) is used to enable students with relevant certificated prior learning to be admitted with credit to a new programme of study. In many cases the prior certificated learning will be a certificate, such as an HNC/D, that is used frequently as admission with credit and for which the university processes will be relatively straightforward. It is likely that such qualifications will be recognized by the university on a 'once and for all' basis as admission with credit at a particular value to a particular programme. However, as credit transfer activity has increased, and is better understood by both students and receiving institutions, the range of certificated learning presented has become more diverse. This is considered below.

A student might have an award such as a Certificate in Religious Computing from Metropole Theological College that has not previously been credit rated by Modcred University. The student may want to use this for the purposes of admission with credit to the BSc(Hons) Computing Studies at the University. How much credit, and at what level, does this award carry in relation to the degree and how are these decisions arrived at?

Modcred University established a staff development programme to ensure that all admissions tutors were aware that the processes for *admission with credit* are fundamentally different from those of *advanced standing* which they replaced. Staff came to appreciate that admission with credit gives credit for relevant learning already achieved and must therefore be recorded on the student record and transcript as credit earned in the same way as any other credit. (This is philosophically and procedurally different from the notion of *exemption from study* that advanced standing conferred. By implication exemption from study fails to recognize the actual value of the learning already achieved and the credit it attracts.)

In the context of admission with credit, the admissions tutor attempts to determine a volume and level of credit based on the similarity between the Certificate and the degree, i.e. the extent to which the learning within the certificated programme of study coincides with that of the proposed new learning to be undertaken. The tutor, the specialist in the field, will make an initial appraisal, but the university will want to be assured that this is appropriate in terms of comparable decisions being taken elsewhere in the university or at other universities. (It would be very problematic if the Certificate in

Religious Computing was rated by the admissions tutor as being comparable in level to a Diploma of HE, if in other institutions it was seen as equivalent in level to a lesser qualification.) The process of ensuring wider comparability is often done by a credit specialist in the university who will:

- have access to a database of credit case law;
- be part of a wider credit evaluators' network;
- have the role of checking out the 'credentials' of the institutions awarding the certificate.

Thus in this case Modcred University's credit evaluator will check out the standing and reputation of Metropole Theological College against the database and/or with colleagues in the network. He may also consult relevant national and international reference works. Often this task is simple, but occasionally a great deal of detective work is required, especially where little known overseas institutions are concerned.

It is through the process of combining the judgments of a general *credit specialist* at university level and a subject specialist at 'course' level that the important distinction between *general* and *specific* credit comes to the fore. In practical terms the admissions tutor for computing completes the University's Individual Admission with Credit form which is the first stage in the approvals process. Following endorsement by the credit evaluator this is then forwarded to the University Credit Approvals Board (UCAB). If approved, the credit decision becomes case law and is entered on the database, so that any further applications from students of Metropole Theological College, with this particular certificate, can be dealt with rapidly. It is also essential for that decision to be notified to the student records office so that when the student comes to graduate, his/her credit transcript contains all the APL details and the IT system does not reject the student for not having completed sufficient credit for the degree in Computing Studies.

Modcred University admissions tutors do not have to wait until a student knocks on their door with an APL claim. For many degree programmes there will be well known lower awards which many students will want in the future to use as admission with credit. Thus, for example, the British Computer Society Part 1 award will have been credit rated in the expectation that a number of part-time students will be likely to propose it as the basis of an admission with credit claim. It becomes necessary to present these for approval on a 'once and for all' basis. On the other hand, few computer staff would have expected a claim from Metropole Theological College in advance of it being made.

One way in which the credit rating of well established qualifications is sometimes done is through the standard course *validation* procedures of the University. Thus when the degree in Computing Studies was put forward for validation, a list of qualifications likely to be proposed for admission with credit could have been put forward. This is not, however, the process operated by Modcred University. It takes the view that this is not the best way of maintaining standards since it leads to fragmented outcomes, especially since validation is devolved to faculties and departments. Validation panels rarely have time and expertise to look into these issues of credit effectively. This approach is likely to lead to inconsistent decisions about level and volume of credit. Because APL is not simply advanced standing, but is a refined statement about equivalence, it needs to be managed in a rigorous and transparent way.

The way in which this is done at Modcred University is for the course team to specify the BSC Part 1 and similar awards and, taking advice from the University's credit evaluator, submit the proposed awards (via a Specific Credit Recognition form), through the University's procedures for evaluation by an *independent* 'expert' assessor. This expert assessor will in turn submit a report which will be received by the University's quality assurance body (UCAB). Approval through this central quality assurance mechanism guarantees consistency, transparency and accuracy of records.

### APEL

The practices behind APEL claims must be as rigorous as those for APL especially since there is no certification from any other awarding body to legitimize the learning that a student might be claiming against the new learning proposed. (It should be noted that students making substantial claims for APEL often incorporate a claim for APL as part of the same claim.)

The student will make an initial inquiry somewhere in Modcred University. The University has taken the view that because of the complexity of the processes and of the standards issues involved, this should be a centralized operation. It ensures, however, that the activity related to evaluating experiential claims draws heavily on the subject expertise at departmental level. It recognizes that these first enquiries need personal contact since much effort can be wasted if potential students make speculative claims which have no chance of success. Once it is recognized that there is the basis for a claim, students are given written guidance on the process and asked to complete an Initial Profiling form on which the student outlines the areas of experience against which they feel a claim for credit is viable. At this stage certificated learning bids can also be made so that opportunities for APL claims can be assessed and processed in parallel. After initial scrutiny, which demonstrates the viability of the proposal, the student, under the supervision of an APEL tutor/adviser, starts developing the means of demonstrating their experiential learning for which credit is to be claimed. At Modcred University, as in most universities, this is demonstrated through a portfolio which is sometimes supplemented by additional or alternative methods of evidencing and/or assessment. The University also offers taught and self managed modules (which are themselves credit bearing), that are designed to enable students to develop their claims in the most effective way.

On completion the portfolio (which might be lengthy) is accompanied by an APEL Summary statement, which summarizes the content of the claim and the proposal for credit volume and level. The University then makes an appraisal. This is done in a number of ways but normally the APEL tutor makes a preliminary recommendation, which alongside the portfolio goes to an independent assessor who completes a report. Modcred University expects the internal APEL adviser to require revisions to the claim if necessary prior to making their recommendation to the University Credit Approvals Board (UCAB). It considers that this is very important in maintaining the integrity of the award and process, since claims on the basis of learning from experience are being used to replace credit that would otherwise derive from taught university modules. The final stage is for UCAB to make its decision about whether the student should be allowed to forego course content on the basis of previous experience from which learning has been derived. To do this effectively it is helpful for the APEL summary, the tutor's recommendation and the views of the independent assessor to be considered at the same time. All decisions made at UCAB are recorded on the student record system to avoid problems at the point of conferment of the award.

In conclusion it is worth noting three key points about the way in which Modcred University's record system records credit that derives from prior learning. Firstly, the method is applied *without exception* across the institution. Secondly, it is recorded as APEL credit (without implying that it is qualitatively different from credit derived from conventional taught programmes). Thirdly, the credit is itemized in order to give full details of the learning derived from APEL on the student's transcript which accompanies the degree certificate.

# In-company Accreditation[1]

This case study concerns the 'accreditation' of education and training provision in a local authority. It is a particularly good example in that it demonstrates how development of the accreditation programme eventually resulted in a wider partnership between the university and the 'company'. It does not contain any standard accreditation of existing in-house 'training', although it was expected at the outset that this would be a possible outcome. In the event the needs of the local authority were best met through adaptation and re-purposing of existing university provision with special arrangements made for delivery. In our experience this is fairly common. Increasingly, there is no such thing as a 'typical' in-company accreditation. They are all different, the common thread is the application of the flexible processes of the University (made possible through CBMS) to enable a quality assured, academically viable response to customer need.

The local authority had called in a consultancy team some 18 months prior to contacting the University. It had been working with the consultants to plan a business process re-engineering programme, with three main aims:

- streamlining;
- de-layering;
- improvement in customer focus;

to make the local authority more responsive to customer needs and to be more customer-friendly.

To work successfully, an important requirement for the de-layering and streamlining was a training programme for middle managers, concentrating on five themes:

- Teaching and learning, the learning organization, study skills;
- Local government;
- Management, including empowerment;
- Quality;
- Self development, including individually chosen options such as 'numeracy', and 'improve your reading' at one end of the scale, to 'strategic financial planning' at the other end.

Finally, at this points, the local authority and consultants had agreed on four levels for the training programme, and had begun to identify providers, titles, syllabi etc.

All of this work had been progressing internally in the local authority. Modcred University was first approached in late January, with an intended start point for the programme in September of the same year. While some might consider this a short lead time, it is not untypical and one to which a CBMS institution can respond relatively easily. The first contact centred around the consideration of a folder of proposals, which consisted of a grid of levels and the themes described above. There was an incomplete set of intended 'module' details presented to the University, in a range of styles. (Some were from the BTEC Professional Development Award, some were NVQ attainment statements, some were written in-house, and some were simply a title expressing an idea.) The situation at this point was complicated by the programme being notionally built around BTEC guidelines, which allows for 30, 60 and 90 hour modules, whereas all modules of Modcred University are in multiplies of 75 hours. Many questions were posed by the client to the University namely: How much of this could you do for us? Are there any significant gaps which you could not fill? How can you assure the quality of your accreditation/provision? Have we got the levels right?

At the first meeting it was important to separate out the issues and address them in a logical order. Level was considered first. It became clear that:

1   four levels would not be enough to cover everything from basic numeracy and literacy, to strategic planning which implied postgraduate studies. (Five were subsequently agreed.)
2   the lower two levels as presented would be better handled by the local FE College, so they were immediately discounted from the rest of the discussion. (However, the Modcred adviser contacted the University's regional FE partner in order to facilitate further discussion.)
3   the client was in danger of confusing level of a programme, the volume of study in a module, and also, to a certain extent, the quality of the student's response to assessment.

Following the meeting these issues were clarified in a detailed letter which set down on paper an agreed meaning of the terms to be used by the partners and as applied within the University. It also contextualized the levels to be used, by comparing them with other more commonly understood qualifications such as GCSEs, 'A' levels, Higher National Certificate, etc. This letter formed the basis for the next meeting, which also involved a representative from the FE College. The meeting agreed definitions of level, the appropriateness of certain approaches to teaching and learning for different groups, and qualifications which might accrue.

The next stage was to attempt to match the titles and topic guides which the client had originally produced with standard modules of the University, ignoring for the moment the differences in total learning hours for each module. It was found that some content specified by the client was covered in existing University modules, along with material not specified in the original plan but, through discussion, seen to be important additional learning. (Other material within existing modules was firmly discounted, particularly in relation to the local government focus required.)

Real progress was made during a series of breakfast meetings involving the University Accreditation Adviser, the Business Development Manager from the University Business School, the local authority Training Manager and Deputy. A considerable amount of iteration was conducted by post. By the middle of the summer a scheme comprising the accreditation of some in-house provision, together with five University modules at each of the two levels, had been developed. A further 22 customized modules were in preparation. Similar provision at the three lower levels, was being handled simultaneously by the FE College.

Whilst this academic development activity was taking place, the local authority was preparing to launch and promote the new training and development programme. Acceptance of the training programme as a whole, with a large uptake, was seen as vital. This resulted in all partners in the programme taking part in a high profile launch day, on the council's premises, where employees could receive guidance and advice from Modcred University staff, FE staff, and the council training department staff. This resulted in over 50 council staff indicating they would wish to enrol on University modules.

These people were subsequently invited to an induction day at the University, held on the 1st October, only seven months after the first contact had been made. Again, these events were planned to dovetail in with a similar one being held at the FE College. At the University induction day, 54 people enrolled for between one and five modules, with delivery beginning the next week.

Since the initial delivery cycle, several modifications have been made to the programme to meet the needs of the client. Furthermore, the University has agreed to develop material at the 'missing' level (the University's level 1) since the programme participants have identified that there is a gap between the FE provision and the University's.

In summary, this accreditation exercise resulted in two 50 credit named awards being created specifically for the client, the adaptation or bespoke design of 22 modules at HE levels 2, 3 and 4, delivered largely but not exclusively by University staff, backed up by a five year agreement to provide these modules, updated as necessary, to the client group. This brought in considerable income to the University. Additionally, there is a development team working on both undergraduate and postgraduate awards in 'Public Sector Management', as a progression route for students who wish to continue their studies to gain a standard HE award.

## Note

1   We are indebted to our colleague Bob Mercer for providing this case study.

# Bibliography

ALLAN, J. (1996) 'Learning outcomes in higher education', *Studies in Higher Education,* **21**, 1, March.

ASSOCIATION OF GRADUATE RECRUITERS (1993) *Roles for Graduates in the Twenty-first Century,* Cambridge: AGR.

ASSOCIATION OF GRADUATE RECRUITERS (1995) *Skills for Graduates in the Twenty-first Century,* Cambridge: AGR.

BADLEY, G. and MARSHALL, S. (1995) *53 Questions and Answers about Modules and Semesters,* Bristol: Technical and Educational Services Ltd.

BARNETT, R. (1997) *Realizing the University* (Inaugural Lecture), London: Institute of Education.

BILLING, D. (1996) 'Review of modular implementation in a university', *Higher Educational Quarterly,* **50**, 1, January.

BRENNAN, J. and LITTLE, B. (1996) *A Review of Work-based Learning in Higher Education,* London: QSC/DfEE.

CHALLIS, M. (1993) *Introducing APEL,* London: Routledge and Kogan Page.

CONFEDERATION OF BRITISH INDUSTRY (1989) *Towards a Skills Revolution,* London: CBI.

COUNCIL FOR NATIONAL ACADEMIC AWARDS (1989) *Credit Accumulation and Transfer Scheme: Regulations for Students Registered Centrally with the CAT Scheme,* London: CNAA.

COUNCIL FOR NATIONAL ACADEMIC AWARDS (1992) *Academic Quality in Higher Education: A Guide to Good Practice in Framing Regulations,* London: CNAA.

DEARING, R. (1997) *Higher Education in the Learning Society: Report of the National Committee,* London: HMSO.

DfEE (1998a) *The Learning Age* (Cm 3790), The Stationery Office: HMSO.

DfEE (1998b) *Higher Education for the 21st Century:* London: HMSO.

DfEE (1998c) *Further Education for the New Millenium: Response to the Kennedy Report,* London: HMSO.

EMPLOYMENT DEPARTMENT (1990) *The Skills Link,* Sheffield: Employment Department.

EMPLOYMENT DEPARTMENT (1992) *Learning through Work,* Sheffield: Employment Department.

EVANS, N. (1994) *Experiential Learning for All,* London: Cassell Page.

FRYER, R. (1997) *Learning for the Twenty-first Century,* London: NAGCELL.

FULLAN, M. (1991) *The New Meaning of Educational Change,* London: Cassell.

HARVEY, L., MOON, S. and GEALL, V. (1997) *Graduates Work: Organisational Change and Students' Attributes,* Birmingham: CIHE/DfEE/AGR.

HIGHER EDUCATION FUNDING COUNCIL FOR ENGLAND (1996) *Fast and Flexible: The AIRs Experience,* Bristol: HEFCE.

HIGHER EDUCATION QUALITY COUNCIL (1995a) *Graduate Standards Programme: Interim Report,* London: HEQC.

HIGHER EDUCATION QUALITY COUNCIL (1995b) *Guidelines on the Quality Assurance of Credit-based Learning,* London: HEQC.

HIGHER EDUCATION QUALITY COUNCIL (1996a) *Understanding Academic Standards in Modular Frameworks,* London: HEQC.

HIGHER EDUCATION QUALITY COUNCIL (1996b) *Learning from Audit 2,* London: HEQC.

HIGHER EDUCATION QUALITY COUNCIL (1996c) *Strengthening External Examining,* London: HEQC.

HIGHER EDUCATION QUALITY COUNCIL (1997a) *Regulatory Framework for Assuring Academic Standards in Credit-based modular Higher Education — Graduate Standards Programme,* London: HEQC.

HIGHER EDUCATION QUALITY COUNCIL (1997b) *Graduate Standards Programme: Final Report,* London: HEQC.

HILLMAN, J. (1996) *The University for Industry,* London: IPPR.

KENNEDY, H. (1997) *Learning Works Widening Participation in Further Education,* Coventry: Further Education Funding Council.

OTTER, S. (1992) *Learning Outcomes in Higher Education,* London: HMSO.

ROBBINS, LORD. (1963) *Higher Education (Robbins Report),* Cmnd. 2154, London: HMSO.

ROBERTSON, D. (1994) *Choosing to Change. Extending Access, Choice and Mobility in Higher Education,* London: HEQC.

SEEC (1996) *Credit, Guidelines, Models and Protocols,* Sheffield: DfEE.

SMITHERS, A. and ROBINSON, P. (1995) *Post 18 Education: Growth, Change, Prospect,* The Council for Industry and Higher Education, Executive Briefing.

THEODOSSIN, E. (1986) *The Modular Market,* Bristol: The Further Education Staff College.

TRADES UNIONS CONGRESS (1989) *Skills 2000,* London: TUC.

TROWLER, P. (1996) 'Angels in marble? Accrediting prior experiential learning in higher education', *Studies in Higher Education,* **21**, 1, March.

UNIVERSITIES AND COLLEGES ADMISSIONS SERVICE (1996) *Accreditation of Prior Learning: Briefing for Higher Education,* Cheltenham: UCAS.

WILLIAMS, G. (1997) 'Editorial', *Higher Education Quarterly,* **51**, 1, January.

WINTER, R. (1993) 'Education or grading arguments for a non sub-divided Honours degree'. *Studies in Higher Education,* **18**, 3.

WINTER, R. and MAISCH, M. (1996) *Professional Competence and Higher Education: The Asset Programme,* London: Falmer Press.

WOOLLARD, A. (1995) 'Core skills and the idea of the graduate', *Higher Education Quarterly,* **49**, 4, October.

# Index